Risdon Bennett

The Diseases of the Bible

Risdon Bennett

The Diseases of the Bible

ISBN/EAN: 9783337097479

Printed in Europe, USA, Canada, Australia, Japan

Cover: Foto ©Lupo / pixelio.de

More available books at **www.hansebooks.com**

Oxford

PRINTED BY HORACE HART, PRINTER TO THE UNIVERSITY

By-Paths of Bible Knowledge.

IX.

THE

DISEASES OF THE BIBLE.

BY

SIR RISDON BENNETT, M.D., LL.D., F.R.S.

Second Edition, Revised.

THE RELIGIOUS TRACT SOCIETY,

56 PATERNOSTER ROW, AND 65 ST. PAUL'S CHURCHYARD.

1891.

PREFACE.

---·---

ONE of our most illustrious physicians, distinguished alike as an accomplished scholar and patron of learning and the arts, Dr. Richard Mead, Court Physician to George II, was the first British author who published, towards the end of his busy life, a distinct and scholarly work on the Diseases of the Bible, entitled *Medica Sacra.*

The original edition was in Latin, in the preface to which he says, 'Βεβήλοις autem hæc non scripsi ; sed iis tantum qui aut sacris theologicis aut medicis, initiati sint et eruditi.' For neither of these classes are the following pages primarily intended, but rather for the ordinary educated student of the Scriptures, whether professional or not. The subject, however, involves the discussion of questions demanding the aid of both the initiated and the learned. I have endeavoured to abstain as much as possible from either method or language that would not help the general reader, and have confined myself mainly to the medical aspects of the subjects discussed.

To my friends, Dr. W. A. Greenhill and the Rev. Dr. Green, my grateful thanks are due for the assistance which they have kindly afforded me. To Dr. Greenhill, not only for the benefit which I have derived from his published writings, but also for the valued criticisms and help with which he has favoured me while these sheets have been passing through the press; to Dr. Green, for the needed aid of his Hebrew scholarship.

CONTENTS.

INTRODUCTION.

To every sincere believer in Divine revelation it must be a matter for unfeigned thankfulness to find how much has been done in recent times to harmonise Scriptural records with the present state of natural science, as well as to show how unreasonable it is to adduce objections based on brief incidental references to subjects of which but little was known when those records were penned. But whatever may be the relation between Scriptural teaching and physical or any branch of natural science, the reader of the Bible cannot fail to be struck with the relation between theology and medicine which is manifest both in the Old Testament and the New. The connexion between sin, which 'brought death into the world and all our woe,' so abundantly shown in the Old Testament, and forgiveness of sin and the 'healing of all manner of sickness and all manner of disease among the people,' so wondrously portrayed in the New, as characterising the Saviour's sojourn on earth, seem not only to warrant but to demand a careful study of those diseases which are mentioned in Holy Scripture, as viewed in their human aspect and in the light of modern medical science.

In the following pages an attempt is made to investigate and illustrate the nature and course of some of the diseases particularly mentioned in the Bible, but not to give either a complete Biblical nosology or an account of Hebrew medicine.

It is indeed remarkable how little is said of the treatment of disease and how much of its prevention. Sanitary laws are laid down in the most specific and detailed form, and the Mosaic sanitary code may be said to constitute the basis of modern sanitary legislation. Rules relating to food, clothing, personal cleanliness, intercourse with the sick and contact with the dead, and various matters connected with social life, are given in minute detail, the value and import of which it is for the most part easy to see.

In what is said of those forms and particular examples of disease of which we have treated, no attempt is made always to discriminate between the different means by which, or purposes for which, they were inflicted. In some cases they appear to have occurred as ordinary calamities, as in that of the child of the Shunammite woman, caused by exposure to the heat of the sun. In some they were inflicted simply as signs, as in the case of the leprosy of Moses, and were of temporary duration. In others they were evidently brought about by direct Divine intervention, as a punishment for sin, either of individuals or of the people at large. This, in some instances, was made manifest by prophetic warning and threatening.

But though natural laws may, in most cases, have been maintained, these and every human element were manifestly subject to the Divine will. Hence it may not always be easy to say what we are to designate as miraculous, and what we may explain by natural law. We have, however, abundant evidence that in all cases the mitigation and removal of disease were in the hands of Him 'who healeth all our diseases,' as well as 'forgiveth all our iniquities.' In at least one instance we have a distinct reprobation of the non-acknowledgment of this, in the case of Asa, who, 'when his disease was exceeding great, sought not to the Lord, but to the physicians'[1]—relying solely on human means. And of the inadequacy of these means alone we have an example, if any be needed, in the case of the woman with the issue of blood, 'who had spent all her living upon physicians, neither could be healed of any.'[2] But that human means are both sanctioned and enjoined is evident, and there is nothing that would justify either a culpable neglect of human aid, or a recourse to superstitious observances. There appears, however, to have been a tendency in the Hebrew mind, as with the Assyrians and other Orientals, to refer afflictions to evil spirits, which must be borne in mind, especially when considering the subject of demoniacal possession. When nothing is distinctly stated to the contrary, we are justified in assuming that the diseases, whether inflicted in the ordinary course of Providence or not, were subject to the same ordinary laws as those of the present day.

Some of the diseases mentioned in the Bible are simply named, or so briefly described, that we can only surmise what they were. And with regard to others it will be well to admit *in limine* that the most learned physicians of the present day find it difficult to identify them with any particular forms of disease with which they are familiar. Nor can this be matter of surprise, both because the diseases in question were described, in the Old Testament at least, by non-professional writers, and at a time when nothing deserving the name of medical science existed; and also because diseases alter much in their characteristics with lapse of time and change of

[1] 2 Chron. xvi. 12. [2] Luke viii. 43; Mark v. 26.

climate and environment, some, there is reason to believe, disappearing altogether. This more especially applies to such cutaneous diseases as are delineated, however minutely, in Lev. xiii. and xiv. The case, however, is different when we come to the time of the New Testament and of Greek and Arabian medical writers, whose descriptions are, for the most part, such as are readily recognised.

In Egypt the priests acted as physicians, and appear to have had special diseases, as well as special duties, assigned to them. Some, for example, had diseases of the eye, and some those of the ear,[1] allotted to them, and some the duties of embalming. Thus we are told that 'the physicians embalmed Israel.' They were a very numerous body, and formed part of the retinue of the great. They must certainly have acquired some knowledge of anatomy, if only from the process of embalming, together with some experience of diseases and the use of surgical instruments. The Egyptian priests had their canons of practice, as laid down in their sacred books, which they were bound to obey. But such rules of practice consisted largely of superstitious and ceremonial observances. The chief priest-physicians, the Magi, the wise men and magicians of whom Moses speaks, claimed superhuman powers in the control of diseases.

That the Hebrews obtained what knowledge of disease they had mainly from the Egyptians there can be no doubt, and this would appear to have fallen naturally to their own priesthood. For although the Jewish priests were not *ex officio* physicians, they evidently had to do with matters of sanitary and medical science. And we

---

[1] Specimens of *ex voto* tablets given by Wilkinson afford curious evidence of this.

may safely assume that Moses, who 'was learned in all the wisdom of Egypt,'[1] would not be deficient in such knowledge of disease as the Egyptians possessed. But how much or how little this amounted to we cannot tell, notwithstanding the flood of light which, in recent times, has been shed on the manners and customs of the Egyptians, and the evidence we have of their use of remedies and of the reputation in which they were held as medical practitioners in historic times. Nor must we overlook the evidence, scattered and slight though it be, of medical, or at all events surgical, knowledge possessed by the Hebrews in patriarchal times.

It is also deserving of notice that neither in the Levitical laws, nor elsewhere in the Old Testament, is there any mixing up of cures and curative means with the necromantic or superstitious observances which form so prominent a feature in the medical practice of all other people in primitive times. It is Jehovah that healeth (Ex. xv. 26), 'Who forgiveth all thine iniquities, and healeth all thy diseases' (Ps. ciii. 3); Who 'bindeth up the breach of His people, and healeth the stroke of their wound' (Isaiah xxx. 26). The wand of Moses and the brazen serpent constitute no exceptions to this statement, as it is evident that to God alone were the miraculous effects attributed.

From what we know of the geographical features of the country, as well as of the customs and trades, we might safely assume that certain kinds of disease would be likely to prevail, and among these would be certain fevers and cutaneous diseases. And although it would not be quite safe to infer, from the accounts of the Egyptian diseases given by the Greek, Arabian, and

[1] Acts vii. 22.

Roman medical writers, that the same diseases, having the same characteristics, existed in the time of Moses, yet they are the highest, as well as the most ancient authorities, to which we can appeal on the questions we have to discuss. The medical terms which they employed as most closely corresponding with the Hebrew text must be allowed to have the utmost weight. And when we come to New Testament times, we have the advantage of reference to Greek and Arabian authorities that is of still greater assistance to us. Physicians then were better instructed and their aid more generally available. So far as we know the history of St. Luke we may take him as an example of one who had had the regular medical education of his day.

The third Gospel and the Acts of the Apostles abound in words and phrases, which for the most part, are not found in the other New Testament writings, but which are common to Greek medical authors. This has been abundantly shewn in the elaborate work of Dr. Hobart, proving from internal evidence that the third Gospel and the Acts were written by the same person, and that the writer was a medical man[1].

[1] *The Medical Language of St. Luke*, &c., by Rev. W. K. Hobart, LL.D. Dublin, 1882.

CHAPTER I.

SECTION I.—*Nomenclature of the Disease.*

SINCE the application of the term *Leprosy* to designate
the disease described in Lev. xiii. and xiv., the greatest
confusion has prevailed in the use of the word, and the
utmost difference of opinion as to what it implies. This
appears to have arisen mainly from the same Latin word,
lepra, having been used in at least two distinct senses.
In the one case it denotes a mere skin disease, and in
the other a serious constitutional malady, having indeed
important cutaneous manifestations, but implicating the
whole organism, and ending invariably, it is believed,
in death. When used originally to denote simply a
disease of the skin, *lepra* was synonymous with the
Greek λέπρα, the radical meaning of which is rough or
scaly (λέπος, a husk or scale). No medical author, it
is believed, either before or after the time of St. Luke
ever used the Greek word λέπρα to denote anything but
some rough scaly cutaneous disease.[1] The old Greek
version of the Pentateuch translates the Hebrew *tsara'ath*
צָרַעַת by λέπρα, indicating thereby that the translators
considered the Levitical disease (called in the Authorised
Version *leprosy*) to be the skin disease known by that

[1] See on this whole subject Dr. Greenhill in the *Bible Educator*,
vol. iv. p. 76 et seq., 1876.

name in Greek medicine. In modern times also, the same word has been applied to one of the forms of scaly skin disease that was called *lepra vulgaris*. This, however, has been abandoned; what was at one time so called being now classed as a variety of psoriasis, an ancient and very common cutaneous disease. It may indeed be said to be the most universal of all skin diseases, being found in every climate and among all races, though most common in equatorial latitudes and among the coloured races. But, as Philo has remarked of λέπρα,[1] it is 'a multiform and complicated' disease, and when differing from its more usual aspect has received special or colloquial names.

How then, it will be asked, came the terms *lepra* and leprosy to be applied to that far more serious and indeed awful disease prevalent in the Middle Ages, and still widely spread through the world, technically called *elephantiasis Græcorum*, and now spoken of as 'true leprosy?' In the present day, this formidable disease is not known as indigenous, either in our own or in some other countries, where it was for several centuries endemic, but is still fearfully prevalent in the East, in the South Seas and West Indian Isles, and in Scandinavia. It was to those who were the subjects of this disease that the terms *lepra* and lepers were applied, in the Middle Ages, when Wycliffe made his translation of the Bible; and to such only are they in the present day applied. A satisfactory answer to the above question is, therefore, a requisite preliminary to any discussion as to the nature and characteristics of the Mosaic disease, as well as to a right understanding of the leprosy of the New Testament.

Dr. Greenhill, in the papers already referred to, traces

[1] *De Poster. Caini,* § 13, tom. i. p. 234, ed. Mangey.

the origin of the use of the word *lepra* in the mediæval sense, as synonymous with elephantiasis, to Constantine, a monk of Monte Casino, who died towards the end of the eleventh century.

The following is Dr. Greenhill's view of the origin of the confusion that has arisen from the misapplication of the terms:[1] 'The Latin word *lepra* is used to signify both the leprosy of the Middle Ages and also the *lepra vulgaris* psoriasis of modern nosologists. We cannot explain *how* it came to be used in two such different senses, but we think we can trace the confusion to its fountain-head; at least we will put together a few points which, so far as we are aware, have hitherto escaped observation, and which appear to us to be not unworthy of the attention of the medical antiquary and his- torian. The treatise which appears among the works of Constantinus Africanus, under the title *De Morborum Cognitione et Curatione*, is known to be a translation of an Arabic work by Ibn-el-Jezzar, who lived in the tenth century. This work also exists in Greek and Hebrew, and therefore enjoys the honour (unique probably) among the older medical writings of being found in no less than *four* different languages.

'In this work the chapter on the Arabic *judhâm* or *true leprosy* is headed Ἐλεφαντίασις in the Greek MS., and *De Elephantiasi* in Constantine's printed Latin version (p. 160), but in the body of the chapter the disease is called *lepra*, which is probably the earliest Latin instance of the word being applied to ἐλεφαντίασις. Why he should have used two different words, and not synonymous, to designate the same disease we cannot

[1] *British and Foreign Med. Chir. Review*, vol. 54, p. 117.

B

tell.' We know also that from the close similarity of certain skin diseases, especially those coming under the category of the old Greek λέπρα, with some of the cutaneous manifestations of elephantiasis or modern true leprosy, the subjects of various skin affections were often erroneously considered to be leprous, and treated as such by confinement in leper hospitals. In this way the popular confusion would be maintained. To such an extent was this the case, that when, in the beginning of the sixteenth century, an inspection was undertaken in France and Italy of the overcrowded leper hospitals, the fact came out that, in many of them, by far the greater number, and in some instances the whole of the inmates, were found to be suffering merely from various skin diseases, and only a minority from true leprosy.[1]

In like manner, in the present day, some persons are met with in India who are deemed lepers, but are not treated as such, either from being considered to have the malady in a mild form in which the chief visible sign is a persistent skin disease, or because they really have only some analogous skin affection, such as *leuco-derma*.

We may now then, without entering too much into medical details, which would scarcely be acceptable to

---

[1] Hirsch, *Handbook of Geographical and Historical Pathology*, vol. iv. p. 8. Syd. Soc. Ed. This admixture is not surprising, for in the sixteenth century *lepra*, as the Latin synonym of the Greek, was the word used by medical writers to designate the common skin disease. Thus Mercurialis, *De Morbis Cutaneis*, etc., Venetiis, 1585, chap. v. *De Lepra*, correctly describes the disease in accordance with Greek authorities whom he quotes. One part of his description deserves notice as bearing on the sense to be attached to the description, Lev. xiii. 14–16: 'Lepra aspera est ad contactum, pruritum inducit quandoquidem cutis sola affecta est, *et ideo excoriata ipsa cute caro subiecta sana apparet*.' Oribasius, commenting on the confusion existing in his day, says, 'Vulgus medicorum, Arabas in hoc secuti, lepram cum elephantiasi confundunt, imo lepram pro elephantiasi accipiunt.'

the general reader, briefly describe the two diseases
which have been so unfortunately confounded the one
with the other.

SECTION II.

Lepra of the Greeks and the Modern Psoriasis.

The first, the λέπρα of the Greek physicians (the modern
psoriasis, formerly called *lepra vulgaris*), whence have
been derived the Latin *lepra* and *leprosus* and the English
leprosy, *leper* and *leprous*, is a cutaneous disease varying in
its features, but the essential characteristic of which is a
rough, scabrous or scaly eruption on the skin, with more or
less evidence of surrounding redness or superficial inflammation. This may be limited to particular regions, though
rarely seen on the face, or may extend over the greater
part of the body. These scaly patches assume different
forms, some being more or less circular with depressed
centres. In some the surrounding edges are more or
less elevated. The patches vary also in colour, some
presenting a glistening mother of pearl whiteness, others
various shades of a dark colour, grey or purple. These
patches, though for the most part thin, scarcely rising
above the surface of the skin, obtain in some varieties
a thickness that elevates them a quarter of an inch or
more above the surrounding skin.

In severe and protracted cases the surface of the skin
becomes excoriated and exudes serum and blood, which
with the scales may form thick scabs.

If the parts affected are naturally covered with hair,
this for the most part falls off, or becomes thin and
white, or woolly. Of this disease, thus characterised
in general terms, various modifications or varieties are

met with, which have received particular names, and which correspond more or less closely with those employed by the Greek writers, such as λέπρα ἀλφός, λευκή, μέλας. All the species or varieties comprehended under the old Greek generic term λέπρα are in the present day, by very general consent, at least in our country, classed under the head of *psoriasis*, whilst by universal consent, all the world over, the terms *lepra* and *leprosy* are now restricted to the disease called by the Greeks *elephantiasis*. There is no reason whatever to believe that any of these varieties of the old Greek λέπρα (*psoriasis*) are contagious, nor are they ever so treated by physicians in the present day. In the more aggravated and persistent forms they are indeed sufficiently repulsive in aspect to interfere with social intercourse, and when met with in the poor and uncleanly they are apt to be associated with other and infectious disorders, more especially scabies or itch. And it is tolerably certain that the itch existed in Egypt.[1] Nor is *psoriasis* in any sense

---

[1] Deut. xxviii. 27, A.V., ' The Lord shall smite thee with the botch (boil, R.V.) of Egypt (ἕλκει Αἰγυπτίῳ ; Hebrew, בִּשְׁחִין מִצְרַיִם), and with the emerods (εἰς τὴν ἕδραν ; Hebrew, וּבַעְפֹלִים), and with the scab (scurvy, R.V.) (ψώρᾳ ἀγρίᾳ ; Hebrew, וּבַגָּרָב), and with the itch (κνήφῃ ; Hebrew, וּבֶחָרֶם) ; whereof thou canst not be healed.' It is difficult to surmise what the botch or boil of Egypt may have been, though some have sought to identify it with elephantiasis. But ψώρᾳ ἀγρίᾳ, which our versions have rendered ' scab ' or ' scurvy,' admit, it has been said, of being rendered, aggravated or malignant psoriasis, though ψώρᾳ is undoubtedly the Greek medical word for itch. Why in the R.V. it should be called scurvy, a totally distinct disease, does not appear. Κνήφῃ, which both our versions render ' itch,' may very well mean some other cutaneous disease attended by itching and irritation, e.g. *prurigo*. Emerods are pretty generally understood to mean hæmorrhoidal tumours, i.e. ' piles.' They are thus rendered by the Vulgate, and uniformly by the Jewish translation.

In verse 35 of the same chapter, 'And the Lord shall smite thee in the knees and in the legs with a sore botch (boil, R.V.), (Hebrew, בִּשְׁחִין רָע ; ἕλκει πονηρῷ), that cannot be healed, from the sole of thy foot unto the top

a dangerous disease, or attended even by any grave or very distressing symptoms, though in severe cases there may be a good deal of irritation, and from accidental causes some of the patches may pass into the condition of open sores or raw spots. Though often very persistent and rebellious to treatment, it is curable, but apt to recur. There is some reason for believing in a hereditary tendency to the disease, and certain constitutions are more liable to it than others. It can scarcely be said to interfere with the ordinary duties of life, or with mental activity, although when associated, as it often is, with other causes of impaired health there may, after a while, be loss of both flesh and strength.

There are several kinds of what are called *epiphytic* skin diseases, i.e. diseases which are produced by vegetable parasites or *epiphytes*. The appearances presented by these have some analogy with those of some of the varieties of *psoriasis*. They are all contagious, inasmuch as they are propagated by the transfer of the particular *epiphyte* from one person to another. The danger of contamination depends, however, very much on the soil, or state of skin and health of the individual, with which the epiphyte is brought into contact. The common ringworm, so troublesome in schools, is a well-known example of such disease. None of them, however, much impair the general health.

There are also various fungi, such as those which give rise to common mouldiness and the dry rot, which are self-propagating, and by which houses and garments are affected. There is little difficulty therefore in understanding what may be meant by leprosy in the house.

of thy head,' the sore botch or boil is probably the same as the botch of Egypt in ver. 27.

or raiment, though the Mosaic description may not enable us to speak with confidence as to the particular species denoted. They for the most part indicate an unwholesome state of the atmosphere where they are found. Some Jewish writers maintain that the marks of house leprosy correspond exactly in appearance with those of the person, but no appearances on inanimate objects can be said to betoken either leprosy or any other malady.

SECTION III.—*Elephantiasis Græcorum.*

Elephantiasis Græcorum, the designation of the other disease to which, as we have said, the term leprosy is now restricted, differs essentially from the cutaneous affections of which we have spoken, both in its nature and general characters. It is one of the most formidable and hopeless of all known maladies. In some respects it may be said to have most analogy with scrofula or syphilis. The term *elephantiasis* seems to have been given to it from consideration of its greatness and gravity. Aretæus,[1] the Greek physician, speaks of it as so much greater than the rest of diseases as the elephant is bigger than all other animals. But the term may, with equal probability, have been given to it from the thickened dense condition which the skin assumes, very like that of an elephant, and its diminished sensitiveness to impressions.[2]

[1] *Morb. Chron.* ii. 13.
[2] Curiously enough, whilst the *Lepra Arabum* is the *Elephantiasis Græcorum*, or true leprosy, the *Elephantiasis Arabum* is a totally distinct disease, known in the present day as the 'Barbadoes Leg.' This is characterised by hypertrophic enlargement of the legs and certain parts of the integuments, associated with a dropsical condition, and is believed to be of malarious origin. This form of elephantiasis, the *E. Arabum*, exists in

Although, according to Dr. V. Carter, the true leprosy in a few rare cases supervenes suddenly, in persons of apparently sound health, its commencement is usually ill defined and its early progress slow and insidious. The earliest symptoms of ill-defined bad health may pass off and recur on several occasions, at various intervals. After a while, two distinct features are manifested, loss of sensibility of the nervous fibres supplying the skin and a congested state of the minute vessels, showing itself in the form of circular spots or blotches of irregular forms and varying extent, on the forehead, the limbs and body, the face and neck perhaps showing only a diffused redness. Even these symptoms may disappear for a time, to return only with increased intensity, the spots assuming a darker or coppery colour; stains appear on the skin, which at length becomes tumid, thickened, and rugous, something like the rind of a rough orange. The central portions of the circular spots, in some instances, turn white, and the whole assumes the character of a white blotch. Thus there may exist at the same time, red, purplish, or white spots, some having elevated edges and of various outlines. The eyebrows, nose and ears, are the parts of the face most frequently affected; elsewhere the spots generally coincide with the distribution of the nerves. The surface of the blotches may be dry and scaly, or moistened by a greasy exudation. In the early stages there is scarcely any pain, and there may not be much throughout, unless from accidental pressure or injury of particular parts; but a certain degree of numbness or *anæsthesia* exists in all the affected spots,

the West Indies and South Sea Islands, and is not infrequently met with, but has never at any time by medical writers been called leprosy. The term elephantiasis seems to have been applied to this from the similarity to the leg of the elephant, which the leg and skin of those affected present.

the fingers especially being numb, wasted and brown. In many even advanced cases its manifestations may be chiefly seen in the skin and mucous membrane of the mouth, the former showing a number of nodules or tuberosities of various size; in other cases, the joints of the members are dislocated and fall off. In others again the most prominent symptoms are the increased loss of sensation and diseased state of the nerves. In the tuberous variety the nodules increase in size and number with each return of the febrile symptoms, ulcerate, and after discharging for a while at length heal, unless very extensive. The mouth, nasal passages and larynx, in severe cases, are similarly affected. The voice becomes hoarse and feeble or is lost; the septum of the nose is destroyed, and the bones fall in. The eyelids, eyes and ears may also be affected in a like manner, the lobes of the ears sometimes enormously enlarged. But we abstain from farther description of the awful and destructive consequences of this terrible disease, by which, in many instances, almost all trace of the human form and aspect may be destroyed by mutilation and disfigurement.[1] In the anæsthetic variety, whilst the loss of common sensation is more pronounced, there are often internal burning and neuralgic pains productive of great suffering and attended by distressing and frightful dreams.

Instances are recorded where the miserable sufferers

---

[1] In a Roman Catholic Manual for Curates it is said that to some lepers the Sacrament cannot be given, because 'Non possunt Corpus Dominicum sic recipere et tractare in ore suo quin rejicerent ipsum, sic multi quibus reciderunt labia et dentes et sunt totaliter corrosi usque ad guttur.' *Manipulus Curatorum.* Bremen, 1577. Thomson, *The Land and the Book,* p. 653, says: 'Sauntering down the Jaffa road, on my approach to the Holy City, in a kind of dreamy maze . . . I was startled out of my reverie by the sudden apparition of a crowd of beggars " sans eyes, sans nose, sans hair, sans everything." They held up towards me their handless arms, unearthly sounds gurgled through throats without palates.'

have survived the loss of more than one limb ; but though life may be protracted for even more than ten or fifteen years, the disease pursues its onward course. It is irremediable by any known human means, and of the witnesses of such appalling sights it may be said : 'Horror ubique animos, simul ipsa silentia terrent' well nigh to the exclusion of pity.

All observation of this terrible malady goes to prove that it comprises a deep-seated general dyscrasia of the system, but where and how it originates are still involved in mystery. For the present we do not enter on the questions of contagion and heredity.

Its former existence in and subsequent disappearance from certain localities and countries, our own among others, have given rise to a very prevalent opinion that it springs from endemic causes, whether malarious or not. Although most prevalent in hot and damp climates, it is rife in the most opposite climes, in Norway, the East and West Indies, and in the South Seas, and although vicinity to the sea-shore has been thought to have some special influence, it is found in inland districts.

Removal from all known or suspected injurious climatic influences, as well as from all insanitary conditions, are admittedly of the first importance as remedial means, and next to these a generous and nutritious diet.

The history of leper hospitals and institutions in the Middle Ages is fraught with the deepest and varied interest. Nowhere has so full and learned an account been given of them as in the Essays of Sir J. Y. Simpson,[1] although he had specially in view their history in Scotland, where they existed, as well as in the border counties, before the year 1200. And the disease con-

---

[1] *Edin. Med. and Surg. Journal*, vols. 56 and 57.

tinued to exist in the Shetland Isles till the middle of the last century.[1] In Scotland the malady was termed the 'mickle ail,' or great disease, and by the old French chronicler Froissart, who visited Scotland in the time of Robert II, it is called *la grosse maladie.* The hospitals, however, were not for the cure of the infected, but charitable retreats, as the disease was considered incurable. Of this a curious illustration is afforded by the case of one Christian Livingstone, tried for witchcraft, against whom one of the gravest accusations was that she 'affirmit that she culd hail (cure) leprosie quhilk the maist expert men in medicine are not abil to do.'[2]

It has been supposed that the leprosy of the Middle Ages was introduced into England by those who returned

[1] Few persons probably are aware of the extent to which leprosy prevailed in the Middle Ages, or of the number of leper hospitals that existed in Europe. Mezeray says, in his History of Philip II, that in the twelfth century, 'Il n'y avoit ny ville ny bourgade qui ne fust obligée de bâtir un hospital pour retirer les lepres.' *Histoire de France*, tom. ii. p. 168. 1645. Muratori gives a similar account of the extent of the disease in Italy: 'In Italia vix ulla erat civitas quæ non aliquem locum, leprosis destinatum haberet.' *Antiq. Ital. Medii Ævi*, tom. iii. p. 53.

[2] Pitcairn's *Criminal Trials in Scotland*, vol. ii. p. 29. The following is a specimen of one of Christian Livingstone's means of cure, in the words of the libel: 'She took a reid cock, slew it, baked a bannock with the blude of it & gaf the samyn to the leper to eat.' As a further specimen of the many sure and certain cures, the following is given by Michael Scott, the Fifeshire philosopher: 'It ought to be known,' he says, 'that the blood of dogs and of infants two years old or under, when diffused through a bath of heated water, dispels the leprosy without a doubt' ('absque dubio liberat lepram'). *De Secretis Naturæ*, p. 241. Amsterdam, 1790.

That the miraculous powers attributed to the relics of saints were employed will readily be assumed. Fosbroke (*British Monachism, &c.,* p. xv) mentions a fountain near Moissac, the waters of which were so medicated by the relics of a saint contained in the neighbouring monastery that crowds of lepers resorted to them, bathed, and were immediately cured. But the waters were not of sufficient virtue to prevent the disease being communicated to the monks, or to save them when attacked. The fountain therefore, according to the confession of the abbot, was shut up in consequence of some of the monks having died of the disease which their famed waters could infallibly remove.

from the Crusades (1096); but there is ample evidence that it existed in the continent of Europe before the time of the Crusades, and Lanfranc, Archbishop of Canterbury in the time of William the Conqueror, founded a hospital for lepers at Canterbury, *ligneas domos ad opus leprosorum.*[1] Other leper hospitals were also founded before the end of the eleventh century.

Although it was chiefly among the lower orders, the 'villeyns,' that the disease prevailed, no class of society was exempt, not even royalty. King Robert Bruce is believed to have died of it. It appears to have been more prevalent among males than among females.

Much has been said on the injurious effects of particular articles of food, such as fish, as well as on the want of others, particularly salt, and generally on modes of living and habits of life, but nothing has been definitely proved. As to all such external causes of this as well as of other diseases, Sir James Simpson has well observed, 'that the investigation of the causes of disease (ætiology) has probably more than any other department of medicine been marked by belief without evidence and assertion without facts.' Recent discoveries in pathological science would doubtless demand some modification of this severe censure, for which, however, there is still too much justification. It is certainly very difficult to ascertain from the multifarious statements of modern observers, with any degree of confidence, what are the true sources of this fearful malady. Dr. Dudgeon gives an abstract of Chinese views of the disease in his Report on Peking, 1875. Among other names given to the disease is 'lai,'

---

[1] *Antiquities of Canterbury*, vol. i. p. 42, and vol. ii. p. 169. There are other historical evidences that the disease existed both in Great Britain and the Continent before the Crusade exodus.

the term applied to the 'mange' in the dog. It is said to arise from three sources—climate, infection, and defective nutrition. Five different forms of the disease are met with. In one, the skin dies, indicated by loss of sensation; in the second, the flesh dies, and no pain is felt on cutting it; in the third, the blood dies and ulceration and pus are formed; in the fourth, the tendons die and hands and feet drop off; and in the fifth, the bones die, the nose is destroyed. Along with this the eyes, lips, and nose become involved. Among the causes specified is 'the air of graves.' The hereditary and infectious nature of leprosy is noticed and terms used expressive of its malignity.[1]

That its unhappy subjects are rendered unfit for ordinary social intercourse has always been admitted, and from Christian benevolent considerations, as well as on medical grounds, they have not been allowed to appeal in vain for that sympathy, care, and alleviation which can only be afforded by segregation in duly appointed and supervised special institutions.[2]

SECTION IV.—*Characteristics of the Levitical Disease.*

This brief and necessarily imperfect sketch of the diseases which we have attempted to describe, will probably have enabled the reader to form a sufficiently correct

---

[1] Surgeon-Gen. Gordon's *Reports*, 1884, p. 150.

[2] The celebrated tractate of Count Xavier de Maistre, entitled *Le Lépreux de la Cité d'Aoste,* gives a most graphic and pathetic account of his interview with a leper confined in an ancient tower in the suburbs of Aosta in 1797, and cannot be perused without the greatest interest, whether by medical or non-medical readers. See also Sir J. Simpson, *Edin. Med. and Surg. Journal*, vols. 56 and 57, 'Antiquarian Notices of Leprosy and Leper Hospitals in Scotland and England,' replete with learned and historical data.

notion of their respective features. We may therefore proceed to enquire what are the characteristics of the disease or diseases spoken of in the Authorised Version of our Scriptures as leprosy, the most detailed description of which we have given us in Lev. xiii. and xiv.

'When a man shall have in the skin of his flesh a rising, a scab, or bright spot, and it be in the skin of his flesh like the plague of leprosy; then he shall be brought unto Aaron the priest, or unto one of his sons the priests:

'And the priest shall look on the plague in the skin of the flesh: and when the hair in the plague is turned white, and the plague in sight be deeper than the skin of his flesh, it is a plague of leprosy: and the priest shall look on him, and pronounce him unclean.

'If the bright spot be white in the skin of his flesh, and in sight be not deeper than the skin, and the hair thereof be not turned white; then the priest shall shut up him that hath the plague seven days:

'And the priest shall look on him the seventh day: and, behold, if the plague in his sight be at a stay, and the plague spread not in the skin; then the priest shall shut him up seven days more:

'And the priest shall look on him again the seventh day: and, behold, if the plague be somewhat dark, and the plague spread not in the skin, the priest shall pronounce him clean: it is but a scab: and he shall wash his clothes, and be clean.

'But if the scab spread much abroad in the skin, after that he hath been seen of the priest for his cleansing, he shall be seen of the priest again:

'And if the priest see that, behold, the scab spreadeth in the skin, then the priest shall pronounce him unclean: it is a leprosy.'—Lev. xiii. 2–8, et seq., A. V.

Here the first difficulty with which we are encountered is manifestly philological : What is the true meaning of the Hebrew words used to describe the diseases, and what are the modern equivalent medical terms? . We are, no doubt, greatly assisted in this enquiry by translations of the Hebrew texts made at a time when medical science had considerably advanced, and when medical terms were used in a definite recognised sense. And though in some cases these terms may have since acquired a different meaning, there is not often much difficulty in determining what the Greek and other ancient medical writers meant by the terms they employed. In answer to the first question, I am fortunate in being able to give the following, with which I have been favoured by so competent an authority as my friend Dr. S. G. Green: '*Leper* and *leprosy* are always denoted in the Old Testament by words derived from one root (צָרַע, *tsara*), the primitive meaning of which appears to be to sting, hence to smite, the root-element in the word expressing narrowness—hence sharpness, and so affliction and distress generally. The word is used alike for the leprosy of Moses (Ex. iv. 6), of Miriam (Num. xii. 10), also for leprosy of a house (Lev. xiv. 44), and of a garment (Lev. xiv. 55). It was evidently a cutaneous disease, at least in one of its manifestations " white as snow," and in house or garment a white surface, e. g. " mouldiness."

' The following are the terms used to denote the appearances or signs of this *tsara'ath* :

Leviticus xiii. 2	a rising	שְׂאֵת	*s'eth*	swelling.
,, ,,	a scab	סַפַּחַת	*sappachath*	gathering.
,, ,,	a bright spot	בַּהֶרֶת	*bahéreth*	fiery (?).
,, ,, 6	somewhat dark	כֵּהָה	*kehah*	dim, faded.
,, ,, 10	quick raw flesh	חַי	*chay*	living flesh.

Leviticus xiii. 18	a boil	שְׁחִין	sh'cheen[1]	inflamed sore.
,, ,, 30	dry scall	נֶתֶק	nétheq	scurf (from a root denoting tearing off).
,, ,, 39	a freckled spot	בֹּהַק	bohaq	white skin eruption.
throughout	plague	נֶגַע	néga	stroke or smiting.'

Dr. Mason Good,[2] and after him Dr. Belcher[3] and others, consider that Moses described three varieties of leprosy, and used *berat* or *bahéreth*, 'bright spot,' as a generic term, two of these, the *berat kehah* and the *berat l'bhanah*, being the severer, or malignant forms, and *bohaq* a more innocent. All these he identifies with the three Greek varieties of λέπρα, and the three varieties of the *vitiligo* of Celsus,[4] which are described by corresponding Greek terms, viz. λέπρα ἀλφός, λέπρα μέλας, and λέπρα λευκή, all of which Dr. Good classes under the head of his *leprosis*, or *lepriasis*, or the modern psoriasis. Other cutaneous blemishes, or blains, Good considers to be mentioned by Moses, as requiring to be carefully watched, being liable to terminate in the malignant form of leprosy. It must, however, be stated that other writers have not been able to satisfy themselves that the Levitical descriptions are sufficient to identify the signs with those which mark the three varieties of the Greek λέπρα. This probably arises principally from differences in the interpretation of the terms employed to distinguish the different cutaneous changes. Thus 'a rising' in Lev. xiii. 2 has been supposed to denote the thickened rough elevations of skin in elephantiasis; and much stress has been laid on this, as strongly supporting the opinion

---

[1] This is the term employed to denote the disease of Job ii. 7, and that of Hezekiah 2 Kings xx. 7 ; Isaiah xxxviii. 21.

[2] *Study of Medicine.* Some of his conclusions have not satisfied all critics.

[3] *Dublin Journal of Medical Science.* 1864.

[4] *De Med.*, lib. v. in fine.

of those who hold that the Levitical disease was elephantiasis. But the word is held by competent scholars to
denote any pimple or vesicle arising on the skin, and to
be co-extensive with what the Greek physicians termed
φλύκταινα. It must also be remembered that in psoriasis
there is often considerable elevation and thickening of
the cuticle.

The word translated scab in ver. 2 is, according to
Mason Good, the dry *sahafati* of the Arabians, derived
from the same root, and which the Greeks translated by
psoriasis. It would therefore indicate a dry scall or
scale, words derived from the Saxon *sceala*, a rough surface. This Saxon *sceala*, Dr. Belcher says, comprised
two varieties, dry and moist, as did also the Arabic
sahafati. Mason Good says that the description ' dry '
in ver. 30 does not occur in the original, which is נֶתֶק
the root of which Dr. Green says denotes tearing off,
Dr. Good therefore takes this to be a variety of humid
scall, and to correspond to *impetigo*, which forms a thick
crust of exuded matter on the beard, that cannot be
removed by shaving, nor without violence or tearing.
The word used by the LXX to translate נֶתֶק is
θραῦσμα, or crust.

That the descriptions of the various forms of skin
disease were intended, not to denote differences in their
nature or pathology, but to enable the priests to discriminate between the clean and unclean forms, is manifest. They were intended purely for practical use. But
that the three forms of scaly eruption to which the terms
bohaq and *baheréth* are applied, do correspond very closely
if not indisputably with the three varieties of the *vitiligo*
of Celsus and of the λέπρα of the Greeks can scarcely be
denied. Thus we have *bohaq* as representing λέπρα ἀλφός,

bahéreth kehah = λέπρα μέλας, and *bahéreth l'bhanah* =
λέπρα λευκή.

It has been said that the appearances described to
guide the Jewish priests relate only to the early stages
of the disease, and cannot therefore be expected to
comprise any of the advanced signs characteristic of
elephantiasis. But a long list of medical writers of the
Middle Ages might be given who clearly describe the
phenomena of elephantiasis, and among these some who
give minute accounts of the various symptoms which
the physician ought to look for when examining suspected persons, and point out the mode in which he
should proceed before venturing to consign a suspected
person to the seclusion of a leper hospital, and thus doom
him for ever to be a despised 'child of St. Lazarus.'
Now the indications laid down for the guidance of the
Jewish priests comprise scarcely any, if any, of those
insisted on by these mediæval writers, although such
indications are carefully divided by these writers into
(1) occult premonitory signs ('signa occulta principio'),
which, though far more decisive than those given by
Moses, are not to be held sufficient to adjudge the
patient for separation, but only as requiring that he
should be carefully watched; (2) infallible signs, which,
though they are such as are not even hinted at by Moses,
require immediate separation from the people ('quibus
apparentibus patiens est a populo sequestrandus'); (3)
signs of the last stage and breaking up ('naufragium')
of the disease, and which comprise those fearful signs
of deformity and mutilation that characterise the most
advanced cases.[1]

[1] Bernhard Gordon, a physician of Montpellier 1309, as quoted by
Simpson in *Edin. Med. and Surg. Journal.*

Guy de Chauliac, a physician at Lyons and Avignon, in the fourteenth century, in like manner speaks of the equivocal and the unequivocal signs denoting all the species of leprosy, but neither does he give any mere cutaneous appearances as decisive of the disease.[1] It has been affirmed that the blanching of the hair on the patches is decisive of anæsthetic leprosy, but this it certainly is not. Dr. Chaplin, formerly Physician to the Leper Hospital at Jerusalem, says, 'In the interest of scientific truth,' 'that white hairs are not a characteristic of anæsthetic leprosy. I speak from knowledge, having, as Physician to a Lepers' Asylum, closely observed that disease during sixteen years.'

The first mention of leprosy is in Exodus iv. 6, where, as a sign given to Moses to satisfy the people that he had been sent by God, he was directed to put his hand into his bosom, and on withdrawing it 'behold, his hand was leprous as snow,' and after repeating the act, and again plucking out his hand, 'behold, it was turned again as his other flesh.'[2]

The sign thus given was no doubt miraculous; but is it necessary to assume that the appearance presented by the hand of Moses indicated either an incurable or infectious disease, in order to convince the people that it was miraculous, as the commentators suppose? The sign was that of a skin disease well known to the people as gradually and slowly manifesting itself, and of a more

---

[1] Quoted by Simpson. The unequivocal signs ('signa univoca') which he gives are—'(1) rotundity of the ears and eyes; (2) thickening and tuberosity of the eyebrows, with falling off of their hair; (3) dilatation and disfiguration of the nostrils externally, with stricture of them within and fœtidity of the lips; (4) voice raucous and nasal; (5) fœtidity of the breath and of the whole person; (6) fixed and horrible satyr-like aspect.'

[2] The Septuagint says merely 'as snow' (ὡσεὶ χιών); the Revised Version, 'leprous, white as snow.'

or less persistent character, as well as difficult of cure. The sudden invasion of such a disease in fully developed form, and its equally sudden disappearance, were quite sufficient to prove its miraculous occurrence; and there is certainly nothing to lead us to think that it was anything more than a local affection implicating the hand.

The next particular example that we have is the case of Miriam (Num. xii. 10). The pillar of the cloud in which the Lord came down and stood in the door of the tabernacle having departed from off the tabernacle, 'behold, Miriam became leprous, white as snow, and Aaron looked upon Miriam, and, behold, she was leprous.'[1] Here it is observable that the same terms are used to characterise the leprosy as in the case of Moses, whose hand became 'leprous as snow.' In both cases the snowy whiteness is the only characteristic that is given us, and in the case of Miriam, as in that of Moses, the sudden manifestation of the disease in the skin in a form that admitted of no question was proof of its miraculous origin. But the Divine interposition for the cure of Miriam, though doubtless also miraculous, does not appear to have been immediate, as in the case of Moses, it would rather seem that she remained leprous for seven days; probably in order that the judgment of God for her sin might be made manifest to the people. The prayer of Moses that she might be 'healed,' not merely cleansed, was at all events answered after her seven days' seclusion from the camp. No mention is made of any cleansing. But the words of Aaron demand especial attention. 'And Aaron said unto Moses [Revised Version], Oh, my lord, lay not, I pray thee, sin upon us, for that we have done

_____
[1] The Septuagint here has λεπρῶσα ὡσεὶ χιών.

foolishly, and for that we have sinned. Let her not, I pray, be as one dead, of whom the flesh is half consumed when he cometh out of his mother's womb.' It is difficult to understand exactly what is meant by these last words. Do they mean, Let her not be as good as dead, like one whose flesh is diseased and corrupted at birth, and who manifestly cannot live? If so, this is almost the only passage which can be cited in support of the theory that the Mosaic leprosy presents any analogy to the modern leprosy, or elephantiasis. Or do the words simply imply that Aaron, seeing how pronounced was the disease,.felt that she never would be cured by ordinary means, and so during the rest of her life would be shut out from the congregation, and civilly dead?[1] That she was rendered ceremonially un-clean is manifest from what follows, and therefore a period of seclusion was enjoined. More on this difficult passage cannot well be said, except that in this instance the disease was inflicted as a judgment of God for sin, whilst in the case of Moses what appears to have been the same variety of disease was inflicted simply as a sign. Had Miriam presented any of the marks of elephantiasis beyond the cutaneous appearance so as to excite Aaron's despairing cry, would they not have been mentioned?

The next cases are those of Naaman and Gehazi. No description of the aspect of Naaman's case is given; it is simply stated that 'he was a leper.' (2 Kings v. 1.) But he was not therefore the subject of an incurable disease in the estimation of the little Israelitish maid, who said unto her mistress, 'Would God my lord were with the

---

[1] We have abundant evidence that in the Middle Ages any one who was adjudged a leper was separated from intercourse with mankind, 'ab hominum conversatione separandus.'

prophet that is in Samaria, for he would recover him
of his leprosy.' Of Gehazi it is said, 'The leprosy of
Naaman shall cleave unto thee, and unto thy seed for
ever. And he went out from the presence of the
prophet a leper as white as snow.' (2 Kings v. 27.)
His, therefore, is a third case; or, if it were the same
variety as that of Naaman, the fourth case of what has been
called white leprosy. But neither in the case of Naaman
nor of Gehazi is there any evidence that the disease was
contagious, and thus rendered them unclean. On the
contrary, Naaman is represented as living at the court
and discharging his duties as general in the army, and
Gehazi as still serving as the attendant of Elisha and
holding intercourse with the king after he had become
the subject of a leprosy that was to cling to him and his
seed for ever, but which did not impair his health so as
to incapacitate him for service.[1]

In the case of Uzziah (2 Chr. xxvi. 19–21) the character
of the leprosy miraculously inflicted for sin is not described ; it is merely stated that it appeared first on his
forehead. But that it was of the severe type and rendered him unclean must be inferred, because he 'was a
leper unto the day of his death, and dwelt in a several
house, being a leper; for he was cut off from the house of
the Lord.'[2]

The remaining instance given in the Old Testament is

---

[1] Josephus speaks of leprosy in a man as 'a misfortune in the colour of
his skin.' 'There are lepers in many nations who are yet in honour, and
not only free from reproach and avoidance, but who have been great
captains of armies and been entrusted with high offices in the common-
wealth, and have had the privilege of entering into holy places and temples.'
Antiq. iii. c. XI, sect. 4.

[2] The first cutaneous manifestation of elephantiasis is frequently on the
forehead ; hence Uzziah's case is thought to support the opinion that this
was really the nature of his leprosy.

that of the four lepers at the gate of Samaria, 2 Kings
vii. 3, of whose leprosy we know nothing, but infer that
it rendered them unclean, and compelled them to dwell
alone without the gates, though evidently it did not
incapacitate them for bodily exertion.

SECTION V.—*Sanitary and Ceremonial Regulations.*

Having thus sought to gather all the light that we can
from the particular cases recorded in the Old Testament,
we proceed to examine the descriptions and regulations
respecting the disease or diseases mentioned in Lev.
xiii. and xiv.

In these chapters it must, we think, be evident even
to the ordinary reader, and certainly to the physician,
that more than one disease is treated of. Certain
symptoms are described, on seeing which, and after
watching their course, the priest declares the patient
to be clean or unclean, as the case may be; and that
this decision does not turn merely on the slight and
limited character or on the extent and severity of the
outward signs is clear. For, strange as it appears, in
chap. xiii. 12, 13 (R. V.) we are told that if the 'leprosy
cover all the skin of him that hath the plague from his
head even to his feet, as far as appeareth to the priest,
then the priest shall look; and, behold, if the leprosy
have covered all his flesh, he shall pronounce him clean
that hath the plague: it is all turned white: he is clean.'
Here again the appearance is that of the white leprosy,
which, however, is styled the plague.

Whilst *tsara'ath* (צָרַעַת) is the word always used
in the Hebrew to denote what in the A. V. is called
leprosy and the plague of leprosy, it evidently was

employed as a generic term, other words being employed to denote, if not varieties, at all events particular aspects of the disease. Not only Dr. Mason Good, as we have seen, but also Dr. Adams,[1] Dr. Greenhill, and others have bestowed much learned pains in endeavouring to identify these varieties with corresponding diseases of the Greek, Arabian and Latin writers. But though it is not in most cases difficult to see the correspondence between diseases with which physicians in the present day are familiar and those described by Greek and other ancient writers, we cannot speak with more confidence than we have already spoken as to the classical names or position that should be assigned to some of the descriptions given by the Mosaic writer as varieties of *tsara'ath* or other analogous diseases. It may, however, without fear of contradiction be affirmed that scarcely any physician of the present day can see in the various features of the disease described in Leviticus anything but varieties of cutaneous disease of some kind. The use of the word λέπρα, as we have remarked, seems sufficient proof that the LXX considered the Hebrew word to correspond with the Greek word which the Latins called *lepra*. The Latin writer Celsus, whilst using another word, *vitiligo*, de-scribes with great accuracy and clearness the several varieties of the Greek λέπρα, which correspond more or less closely with the Mosaic descriptions. But to none of these does Celsus attribute any contagious property, though he does call them foul (*fœda*). And he distinctly states that they are not dangerous, which could certainly not be said of elephantiasis or modern leprosy.[2]

---

[1] *Paulus Ægineta*, Syden. Soc. Trans.

[2] Celsus, *De Medicina*, lib. v. cap. 28, sect. 19 : ' De vitiliginis speciebus, id est, de alpho et melane et leuke,' i. e. the different species of what is

In what then does the distinction between clean and unclean consist, on which the Levitical laws were based? If we suppose that uncleanness ever implied contagiousness, which, in many cases, we are sure that it did not, the only conclusion to which we can come with any confidence is, that in certain kinds of צָרַעַת there was a contagious element, perhaps unknown to the writer, which might be some form of *epiphyte*, or an *acarus*, as in the case of the itch. Such a complication of an otherwise non-contagious disease would, of course, call for sanitary regulations, and render necessary the seclusion of the affected. But, if apart from such considerations any of the species described were in their nature infectious or contagious, we are ignorant of any analogous diseases, either ancient or modern. Nor is there evidence that any of the species presented, apart from the cutaneous signs, any of the essential characters of such a disease as elephantiasis.

There is nowhere any mention or even hint of the characteristic anæsthesia, or loss of sensation, indicating nerve disease, although the examination of the local signs by the priest was evidently of the most careful and minute description. Nor is there anywhere either in the Old or New Testament any passage to show that a leper had been recognised by any of those hideous signs of deformity or mutilation denoting a pronounced case of mediæval leprosy. Even if we admit that the Levitical descriptions are confined to the early mani-

called now psoriasis, and of which he says, 'quamvis per se nullum periculum adfert, tamen et fœda est.' It is observable that elephantiasis is not treated of in this book v, comprising cutaneous diseases, but in his third book, cap. 25, along with such diseases as jaundice and apoplexy. *Vitiligo* is the term used also by Arnobius (fourth century) to denote the Greek λέπρα (*Adv. Gentes*, lib. I. p. 337, ed. Paris, 1836).

festations of the disease, yet inasmuch as distinct statements are given respecting lepers that were abroad and
not secluded, one would have expected some other signs
besides those presented by the skin to have been noticed,
as modern travellers have done. Neither does it seem
probable that none of those who were secluded were
ever seen from a distance and recognised by such
disfigurement as would have excited horror. Nor is
anything said of any service or care being afforded to
those who were unable to take care of themselves. Again,
of those who were excluded from the congregation on
account of their uncleanness, we have no ground for assuming that the disease was ever fatal, as no such instance
is given; or even that they were in all cases irremediably
diseased and never cleansed, whether miraculously, or
by ordinary means employed during their period of
seclusion. On the contrary, the minute rules for cleansing show that they were sometimes cured. If in all cases
the disease was inflicted for sin—of which there is no
evidence—we might perhaps have supposed that the
infliction was irremediable by ordinary means, but not
therefore mortal.

On the other hand, if, apart from all sanitary or
medical considerations, we are to view the disease in a
ceremonial or symbolical aspect alone, it is difficult to
understand either why it should be described at such
length, or why certain species should render the sufferer
unclean, and others not. Why, for example, should one
in whom the leprosy covered all the skin of his flesh,
and who had the plague from his head even to his feet,
be pronounced clean? (Lev. xiii. 12.) That no argument
in support of contagion can be drawn simply from the
sentence of expulsion from the camp is evident from

Num. v. 2–4, and elsewhere, for lepers and non-lepers are equally excluded on the ground of uncleanness. In fact, the laws of seclusion were as rigorously applied to the uncleanness induced by touching a dead body, as well as in other cases where no question of contagion can exist. The same terms are used when speaking of inanimate objects as when speaking of persons, so that Jewish writers have supposed that the same appearances were presented by the spot or eruption in both cases. On the other hand, it must be admitted that from early periods elephantiasis is believed to have existed in Egypt (but whether in the time of Moses we are not certain), and therefore we might assume that the Jews would be likely to be affected. But modern observers who have seen most of *true leprosy* state that it is not very common among Jews. Thus Dr. V. Carter says that during a period of seventeen years, out of a very large number of cases in Bombay, he had seen only four cases and but one death among Jews.[1] The so-called endemic leprosy of Egypt, whatever it was, does not appear to have been known to the older Greek physicians as an Egyptian disease, and the true leprosy or elephantiasis was unknown in the Roman empire till the last century before Christ.

The references made by Brugsch in his *Histoire d'Egypte* to a medical papyrus discovered at Memphis and containing a number of receipts for the cure of disease, 'du genre de la lèpre,' composed during the reign of Rameses II, B.C. 1350, and also to a passage the date of which he throws back to B.C. 4200, do not shed

---

[1] ' In Tangier in the present day the two diseases are found, the *leprosy Hebræorum* prevailing chiefly among the Jewish residents, and presenting exactly the symptoms described in Leviticus. On the other hand, in Syria elephantiasis is unknown among the Jews.' Belcher on *Our Lord's Miracles.*

any real light on the question. The collection of receipts given in the latter document are for curing the *exanthemata*. The way in which Celsus treats the subject of elephantiasis warrants the belief that he, who was not a physician, had never seen the disease, and would explain his omission of the characteristic feature of anæsthesia. He makes no mention of Egypt.[1]

SECTION VI.—*Leprosy of the New Testament.*

In the New Testament twelve cases only of leprosy are mentioned, and ten of these must be considered together under one head. 1. The case of these ten is mentioned only by St. Luke, xvii. 12–19, from whom we might have expected some medical details; but none such are given; the men are simply said to be lepers. But that their disease was of the unclean type we infer, not merely because they stood afar off while lifting up their cry for mercy, but because they were directed to go and show themselves to the priests. It is also deserving of notice that the terms *cleansing* and *healing* seem to be used as synonymous, for as they went they were *cleansed*, before seeing the priests; and one of them, being a Samaritan, when he saw that he was *healed*, turned back to give thanks, glorifying God, and gave occasion to the question of Christ, 'Were there not ten *cleansed*, but where are the nine?' and to His command to the Samaritan, 'Go thy way: thy faith hath made thee *whole*;' without repeating the injunction to show

---

[1] He begins his chapter thus: 'Ignotus autem pæne in Italia, frequentissimus in quibusdam regionibus, is morbus est quem ἐλεφαντίασιν Græci vocant: isque longis *annumeratur*. Quo totum corpus afficitur ita, ut ossa quoque vitiari *dicantur*.' *De Med.* lib. iii. cap. xxv.

himself to the priest.[1] 2. In the case of the single leper that is mentioned in all the three Synoptic Gospels, he is stated to have been in one of the cities with the multitude following the Saviour, and yet is by St. Luke said to be full of leprosy. In this case again the term *cleansing* is used for healing, though the man was enjoined to go and offer for his cleansing according to the law. That St. Luke means by the words 'full of leprosy'[2] that the man was the subject of the severest or inveterate form of disease, and not that he was merely covered with the skin disease, is evident, because in the latter case he would not by the Levitical law have been required to present himself to the priest for *cleansing*. 3. The remaining case, that of Simon the leper, has given rise to much discussion as to how the sitting at meat in the house of a leper could be consistent with Jewish law and custom. Some have sought to solve the difficulty by supposing that Simon was designated 'the leper' merely from having once been leprous for a long time, and known as such. But the more probable explanation seems to be that his leprosy was of the clean type described in Lev. xiii. 12, 13.

From these cases recorded in the New Testament can any inference be drawn adverse to the view that we have taken of the disease described in the Old Testament? Is there anywhere any indication whatever of the sufferers

---

[1] Maundrell, one of the early travellers in Palestine, after mentioning other cases of leprosy that he met with, says: 'At Sichem, near Naplos, there were not less than ten lepers—the same number that was cleansed by our Saviour not far from the same place—that came a-begging to us at one time. Their manner is to come with small buckets in their hands to receive the alms of the charitable, their touch being still held infectious or at least unclean. Their whole distemper was so noisome that it might well pass for the utmost corruption of the human body on this side the grave.' *Journey from Aleppo to Jerusalem*, A.D. 1697.

[2] Luke v. 12, πλήρης λέπρας.

presenting any of the fearful signs of elephantiasis which travellers have noted? In His reply to John's disciples, Christ, recounting His miracles of healing, speaks only of the lepers being '*cleansed*,' and in answering the petition of the single leper He said, ' I will, be thou *clean*,' which seems to convey the impression that removal of ceremonial uncleanness was of more importance than the cure of the disease.

We must again lay stress on the fact that at the time when St. Luke wrote, medical science throughout the East was undoubtedly Greek, though Galen, the great medical authority, was not born till A.D. 130. It seems therefore scarcely credible that St. Luke, himself a physician, should have used the Greek word λέπρα to denote anything but the malady known to physicians by that name, which certainly was a cutaneous disease, but presenting a variety of aspects. Hippocrates (B.C. 460) makes no mention of elephantiasis, but treats of the Greek λέπρα under the plural term λέπραι, indicating thereby that there were varieties, or, as Philo says, that the disease was *multiformis*.

SECTION VII.—*Contagion and Heredity.*

Contagion.—Although it would be out of place in the present work to enter on all the difficult and complicated questions that arise in connexion with the etiology and spread of true leprosy, a few words on these subjects seem required in further elucidation of the view that we have been led to take of the Levitical disease. If we should agree with those who maintain that modern leprosy is not contagious in the ordinary sense, or communicable through contact in ordinary or even intimate social intercourse, it yet might be granted that there is now some reason for believing that by inoculation, or introduction into the system in some other way, as by food or water, an infectious agent may be the means of contaminating the system, and thus be the *vera causa* of disease which might only be developed after a greater or less lapse of time. This latter view would be consistent with the admitted fact, that in but few instances has sufficient evidence been advanced in its support. On the other hand, an overwhelming amount of evidence exists against the spread of the disease by contagion in its ordinary sense, which is quite inconsistent with what we know of other contagious diseases, such as small-pox, which rapidly spread when communicated through the medium of a single infected person. For it is notorious that lepers may be found living for years in populous districts, where never more than a very insignificant proportion ever become affected. Nay, even of leper families a small proportion only may suffer. Such facts also militate strongly against the importance that has been attached to peculiarities of locality, habits and food, notwithstanding the statements that leprosy is almost unknown among the nomadic races.

If, however, we adopt the view that leprosy is another instance of disease induced by the presence of a particular microbe or bacillus, as in so many other diseases now the subject of absorbing interest to both the professional and the non-professional public, we may account for most of the facts adduced in support of the various theories; especially if we admit that there is reason to believe that such microbes, or self-propagating infecting agents, vary greatly in the rapidity with which they permeate the body. For all observers allow that as a rule *true leprosy* is a disease of very slow development—though it is difficult to grant to the incubative stage of a disease thus induced a period of sometimes two or even eight years, which Danielsson and Boeck assume.[1] In the Middle Ages it is certain that the belief in the contagion of the *true leprosy* was very general, both among physicians and the common people; but it is also true that, as medical science advanced and the diagnosis of disease became more definite and reliable, this opinion lost ground and was at length abandoned. On this change of popular belief, Brunelli, an Italian physician, aptly remarks: 'l' opinione era contagiosa e non la malattia.' Hirsch, as the result of his exhaustive study of the disease, says, 'My conviction is that there is not a single fact which tells decisively and indisputably for the conveyance of the disease by contagion.' Is there any single fact in the Levitical record to prove that the same cannot be said of *tsara'ath* so far as regards persons? and is not Brunelli's saying applicable here also? Has not the belief in the contagious character of the Levitical disease originated mainly from two sources—(1) from viewing the terms *clean* and *unclean* as synonymous with contagious and non-contagious; (2) from assuming that the mediæval leprosy was essentially the unclean

---

[1] The following instance has been given in illustration of the doctrine of infection through inoculation, and also of the prolonged period of incubation. Dr. Hillebrand narrates a case in Borneo, where a boy of European parentage was accustomed to play with a leprous child of colour. The native boy thrust a knife into the anæsthetic part of his body, which act was immediately imitated by the white lad, with the same knife. The white lad was soon after sent to Holland, where he grew to maturity, and nineteen years later (!) developed the disease, returning to Borneo a confirmed leper. (*Reports furnished to the Hawaiian Government*, Honolulu, 1886.) A case has also been recently recorded by Dr. T. G. Gairdner, in which a child appears to have been infected with leprosy through inoculation with virus taken from a leprous vaccinifer. *Brit. Med. Journal*, June 11, 1887, p. 1269.

form of *tsara'ath*, translated λέπρα by the LXX and leprosy in the A. V., and adopting the prevalent mediæval belief as to the contagiousness of elephantiasis? From the Mishna it would appear that the Jews did not view even the unclean as contagious, for they allowed an unclean leprous bridegroom to remain with his bride during the nuptial week. Certainly the very general adoption by theologians of leprosy as a type of sin is more likely to have arisen from the analogy presented by the deepseated, all-pervading, corrupting and mortal character of mediæval leprosy,[1] than from anything that is said in the Bible. If, however, none of the forms of *tsara'ath* possessed any such characters, even allowing that some of them were contagious or infecting, there appears no sufficient ground for believing that *tsara'ath* was intended in any special way to typify sin and its consequences, whilst there can be no difficulty in seeing why it should have occasionally been inflicted as a punishment for sin, and made a reason for exclusion from the congregation. For it was a disease of which a person carried about him visible marks of a repulsive character, and perhaps indicative of uncleanly habits. Augustine says that when lepers were restored to health they were *mundati*, not *sanati*, because leprosy is an ailment affecting merely the colour, not the health or the soundness of the senses and the limbs.

The complication of elephantiasis with scabies is not uncommon in Norway, and this, in the opinion of some, has given rise to the belief that the disease in that country is contagious. In like manner the association

---

[1] I have not been able to ascertain the exact date when this very wide-spread notion originated. Dr. Greenhill, however, informs me that the idea has been gen®ral from very early Christian times, [and therefore when λέπρα meant *psoriasis*]. Vide notes at the end.

of scabies with psoriasis (*vitiligo* of Celsus) is mentioned by several Greek authors, and gave rise to the statement of Justin[1] that the Hebrews were expelled from Egypt on account of their ' itch,' though this is admitted to be a slander. In Syria scabies is, in the present day, a much more acute disease than it generally is in European climes, and more rapidly assumes a pustular form, and so gives rise to ulceration.

Heredity.—The subject of heredity is one that is in all cases surrounded with difficulties. There may, however, be said to be a considerable degree of unanimity of opinion in favour of the transmission of true leprosy by way of inheritance. This too was the view entertained by the Arabian and mediæval physicians. But direct transmission from parent to offspring of actual disease or malformations of particular parts, or peculiarities of organization, is one thing, and the transmission of a particular diathesis or disposition to contract particular diseases, which other persons do not possess, is another thing. That true leprosy is transmitted by this hereditary predisposition, if not by congenital seeds of the disease, seems probable. There is but little difference of opinion on the subject, though some observers incline more strongly than others to the belief that there is something more than mere hereditary predisposition, or proclivity to its development in favouring circumstances. Hence the very general adoption of the principle of segregation and the prevention of intermarriages with the healthy.

Is there anything in the history of the Jews, from the time of the Exodus to the present day, to show that they are specially liable either to contract or

[1] *Hist.* xxxvi. 2.

transmit either true leprosy or the various forms of *tsara'ath*? A negative answer must, we believe, be given to this question, although there is reason to think that certain races, particularly the negro race, are specially pre- disposed to elephantiasis. We have cited Dr. V. Carter's experience in India as regards the Jews, but we must not forget the influence of climate and locality in developing the disease *de novo*, of which, however, we have little real knowledge. In certain places, as in Jamaica, the Jews form a large proportion of the sufferers, and it was of the disease there seen and in America that Reill says, ' Lepra Judaica omnino diversa est a lepra Americana.' If racial influences are in any way powerful in the transmission of disease, we might certainly have looked for far more evidence than exists of hereditary tendency to elephantiasis among the Jews, had that been the Levitical disease, especially when we consider that notwithstanding their dispersion they have continued a people apart. And had they any special tendency to contract the disease, it is remarkable that, so far as the writer knows, no case in our times has been introduced by the Jews into this country, to which they come from all the various lands where true leprosy exists, whereas isolated cases have occurred and still occur among British officers and others who have resided where leprosy is endemic.[1]

---

[1] We cannot refrain from making reference to the case of the heroic Father Damien, which has excited so much painful sympathy. This young Belgian Roman Catholic priest, after his ordination in 1873, volun- teered his services in the leper settlement at Malakoi, one of the Sandwich Islands. When he arrived there the lepers numbered 800, of whom between 400 and 500 were Romanists, and were dying from 8 to 12 per week. After ministering to these for 13 *years* (!), in every possible capacity, spiritual and temporal, as doctor, cook, carpenter, and even grave-digger, he has himself fallen a victim to the disease, and has resigned himself with the most

As the result of a prolonged and independent investigation of this much disputed subject, the writer is compelled to admit that he cannot hope to have cleared up all the difficulties with which it is surrounded, whilst on the principal point he has satisfied himself that there is no sufficient evidence that elephantiasis is denoted by any of the diseases described under the head of *tsara'ath*, even if that fearful malady existed in Egypt at the period of the Exodus. Throughout the sacred volume there is no distinctly marked case of elephantiasis described under the name of leprosy, nor any which physicians would have so considered, had not צָרַעַת and λέπρα been translated leprosy at a time when the prevalent mediæval disease was so called. In the main the writer agrees with the conclusions at which his learned friend Dr. Greenhill has arrived : ' That the disease was, in the words of Philo, " multiform and changeful," modified by various complications, and comprising several species more or less distinct ; that some of these varieties were associated with a contagious element, and others non-contagious, and that all the contagious species rendered the patients ceremonially unclean ; that it was not a special or miraculous disease, existing only in those times and countries, but an ordinary malady, used occasionally by God for miraculous purposes; that it was not incurable by human means, though troublesome and obstinate ; that it was not hereditary, though a disease of common occurrence among the Jews.' In further confirmation of the view here taken we may quote the words of Dr. Stapfer, who entirely coincides in the opinion we have formed of the Levitical leprosy, and says that in

touching Christian submission to all its well-known consequences, saying daily to God, ' Fiat voluntas Tua.'

our Lord's time lepers were excluded from the temple,
but not from the synagogue. They had, however, separate
seats assigned to them, and were required to enter first
and leave the last. They were never considered as
'possessed.'[1] Then he says as follows : 'Il est reconnu
aujourd'hui que ces précautions étaient fort exagérées ;
la maladie connue sous le nom de lèpre n'est nullement
contagieuse. Elle peut seulement être héréditaire. Se
présentait-elle sous une forme contagieuse chez les Juifs
de la Palestine ? C'est possible, mais il y avait certaine-
ment beaucoup d'ignorance et de préjugés dans le dégoût
et l'horreur qu'inspirait un lépreux.'. . . 'Non seulement
elle (là lèpre) est guérissable mais elle peut disparaître
sans que le malade suive aucun traitement. C'est une
affection superficielle de la peau, fort peu douloureuse
et qui n'empêche pas la santé générale d'être ordinaire-
ment bonne. Chez les Juifs on distinguait une première
guérison que l'on appelait "purification du lépreux."
Les écailles qui avaient paru sur la peau, et y avaient
formé des disques blancs ou grisâtres, se détachaient et
tombaient. Le malade était dit "purifié" ou "nettoyé."
Sa guérison n'était pas encore certaine, mais le principe
prétendu contagieux avait disparu ; le danger était passé ;
il rentrait dans la vie commune. Son premier devoir
était d'offrir trois sacrifices : le premier était dit d'ex-
piation, et le second de culpabilité ; le troisième était un
holocauste.'[2] The New Testament, the writings of
Josephus, and the Talmuds are the only sources of
information consulted by Dr. Stapfer, and in his opinion
the only ones to be relied on.

---

[1] Negaim, ch. xiii. hal. xii.
[2] *La Palestine au temps de Jésus Christ*, par Edm. Stapfer ; Paris, 1885,
3rd ed., pp. 245 et seq.

Keeping in view the very inadequate evidence of the existence of elephantiasis in Egypt, in Moses' time, apart from what it is sought to derive from the Biblical account of the Levitical disease, we would recommend those who may doubt the correctness of our conclusions to peruse any of the elaborate descriptions of true leprosy in such works as those of Carter and Daniellson, and then, without giving heed to names, carefully peruse the Levitical descriptions, or even merely read attentively such brief sketches of the two diseases as we have given in a previous page, and decide with which the Mosaic account most nearly corresponds.

There is certainly nothing improbable in the supposition, considering the condition of the Jews in Egypt, that they were liable to forms of skin disease, peculiar to the land and their social status, which are unknown to us. It is only quite recently that we have come to know the disease called 'wool-sorters' disease.'[1] And all who are familiar with cutaneous affections are quite aware that the same disease is apt to vary considerably in its outward signs. Seeing the difficulty there is in understanding the grounds for the ceremonial laws of uncleanness in other cases, it is not surprising if we are unable to explain satisfactorily why one form of disease should have rendered a person unclean whilst another form did not. But if we consider such ceremonial laws to have been enacted primarily from sanitary considerations, it is easy to appreciate their value, and also to discern their symbolical meaning and the spiritual instruction thus imparted.

Before leaving the subject of leprosy we feel bound to call attention to the humane and Christian efforts that

[1] See note at the end of the volume.

are being made on behalf of the unhappy lepers of
the present day. Whatever view may be taken of their
disease, it must be admitted that it is essentially immedi-
cable, it is still τὸ πάθος οὐκ ἰάσιμον,[1] that its victims are
the subjects of unspeakable suffering and misery, and that
almost the only hope presented to us for preventing its
spread or exterminating the evil is by segregation and
effectually excluding it from the camp and the congregation. Of the benefits to be derived from segregation
both to the lepers themselves and to the community at
large there cannot be any doubt, whilst we have evidence
sufficient that the sufferers are amenable to Christian influence, and are not beyond the reach of the Gospel of
our Lord and Saviour. We would especially commend
to the notice of Christian philanthropists the efforts made
by the ' Mission to Lepers in India.' The asylums at
Almora, Dara, and elsewhere in India, are entirely supported by this society, and have under care above 100
lepers, at the cost of only about £6 per annum for each
adult. This accommodation is not, however, by any
means sufficient for the districts where the disease prevails.[2]   In Norway, where it is still very prevalent,

---

[1] So called by Cyrill. Alex. in Cramer's *Caten. Græc. Patr. in Nov. Test.*
vol. ii. p. 43.
[2] From statistics in regard to lepers, in the Report rendered to the
Hawaiian Government, it appears that in a total population of 210,767,504
in various countries there were in 1885 124,924 lepers, or 5.9 in every 10,000
of the population. In consequence of a communication from the Under
Secretary of State for the Colonies in 1862, an enquiry was instituted by a Committee of the Royal College of Physicians (of which the writer was a member)
into the whole subject of leprosy, with especial reference to the question of
contagion and the establishment of Leper Asylums. Evidence was obtained
from all our colonies and an elaborate Report made to the Government. From
this Report a mass of authentic and valuable information may be obtained.
The evidence that it affords is decidedly against the contagiousness of the
disease. By a rather singular coincidence the writer is again acting on a
similar committee in consequence of another communication from the

leper hospitals and other less efficient methods of segregation have been proved to be the most efficacious means for diminishing the number of the sufferers. In the Sandwich Islands, where the disease has spread with fearful rapidity, it has been found absolutely necessary to adopt the same means. It is in these islands that the latest observations have been made respecting the presence of specific spores or bacilli in the diseased tissues of the infected; but here too it is found that change of residence to a non-leprous district is one of the most effectual means of exterminating the plague. What are the true etiological relations between microbes and the several diseases with which they are associated we have, however, yet to learn.[1]

Government on the question of the advisability of establishing Leper Asylums and enforcing the principle of segregation. So great is the spread of the disease in many of our colonies, and so persistent is the popular belief in contagion and the necessity for enforced separation of the sufferers, that Government is urged to legislate on the subject and make it penal for a certified leper to be abroad.

[1] See further notes on Leprosy at the end of the volume.

CHAPTER II.

PLAGUE AND EPIDEMIC DISEASES.

SECTION I.—*Plagues.*

SEVERAL Hebrew words are translated by the word *plague* in the Old Testament, and as used in both the Old and New Testament the term is of very wide signification. Indeed, this and corresponding terms, such as *pest* and *pestilence* in modern language, have been employed to denote not only various malignant diseases, but also both moral and physical evil of various kinds. The English word *plague* and the Latin *plaga* are derived from the Greek πληγή, and this from the verb, the radical meaning of which is *to strike* or *smite*. When now used with the definite article to denote the historic fatal form of epidemic malignant fever, it is equivalent to the Greek λοιμός, and to the *pestis* and *pestilenza* of modern language. Hippocrates and the earlier medical writers do not appear to have used the term with precision, as denoting only one form of malignant epidemic disease. But what is now understood as *the* plague or true 'bubo-plague' has characters as distinct as those of small-pox or scarlatina, and may be traced probably as far back as the third century B. C. Oribasius gives a quotation from Rufus, showing that in the time of a physician called Dionysius (about B. C. 277?), a certain disease was known and described as ' pestilentes bubones maxime letales et acuti, qui maxime circa Libyam et Egyptum et Syriam observantur.' And the description which Rufus gives of the disease, as seen by certain physicians in Libya about the time of the Christian era, leaves no doubt as to this being what is now called *the* plague or true bubo-plague. It is therefore probable that this pestilence existed in Egypt even in the time of the Exodus, though there are no sufficient marks given us in the Mosaic record to enable us to identify any of the diseases spoken of as the plague with that which is now so called, and which has from time to time so fearfully ravaged various countries. There is abundant evidence that the word which our translators have rendered by the term *plague* was employed to denote divers calamities and diseases of various kinds, inflicted by God. In Numbers xiv. 37 we read that 'those men that did bring up the evil report upon the land died by the plague before the Lord;' but we have no means of determining what may have been meant by these words, though by the Jews very graphic descriptions have been given of the symptoms in those who died.

In Numbers xi. 31 et seq. we have an account of the mortality that ensued on the eating of the quails given to satisfy the people's lust for flesh. 'And there went forth a wind from the Lord, and brought quails from the sea, and let them fall by the camp, as it were a day's journey on this side, and as it were a day's journey on the other side, round about the camp, and as it were two cubits high upon the face of the earth. And the people stood up all that day, and all that night, and all the next day, and they gathered the quails : he that gathered least gathered ten homers; and they spread them all abroad for themselves round about the camp. And while the flesh was yet between their teeth, ere it was chewed, the wrath of the Lord was kindled against the people, and the Lord smote the people with a very great plague. And he called the name of that place Kibroth Hattaavah, because there they buried the people that lusted.'

The quail (*coturnix*) belongs to the family *Tetraonidæ*, and is still found in Egypt and Arabia Petræa, and indeed throughout the old world. The naturalist Hasselquist considered the bird he saw in Galilee to have special characteristics, and called it *tetrao-Israelitorum*; but Col. Sykes says [1] that our common quail is the identical species on which the Israelites fed, and if so the bird was then, as now, migratory, passing at certain seasons from one country and district to another in search of food. The quail has always been held as a delicacy at table, and was an article of food with the Romans, though Pliny says that there was a prejudice against it, based on the supposition that it was often poisonous, from feeding on hellebore and poisonous seeds, as in our time grouse and other game have sometimes proved to be. Quails are not very abundant with us, only visiting us in the summer; our chief supply comes from France. Vast flocks pass over to the islands and shores on the European side of the Mediterranean, so that methods of wholesale slaughter are had recourse to. There is nothing therefore incredible in the Scripture statement that the birds came with a particular wind in enormous flocks, and covered the ground to a great extent.[2] In verse 33, where the term plague is used, the words admit of being rendered, 'the Lord smote the people with a very heavy stroke,' but the former part of the verse implies that death ensued very rapidly on the

[1] *Zool. Trans.* vol. ii.
[2] Bewick states that they would be driven thither by a south-west wind sweeping over Ethiopia and Egypt towards the shore of the Red Sea.

eating of the longed-for supply of flesh, for the people died 'while it was yet between their teeth, ere it was chewed.' It is therefore quite possible that the birds may have met with deleterious food on their new feeding-ground. But as figurative language, the words may merely imply that the people had scarcely swallowed the food ere they became ill.; and from the description of the enormous numbers of the birds lying on the ground for days in that hot country, it may well be that the flesh was more or less putrid when devoured by the greedy multitude.

The sudden advent of quails in vast multitudes in such a locality, and the great mortality that directly ensued on the eating of them, are quite sufficient to show that it was by 'a very heavy stroke' from the hand of Jehovah that the people perished, that this was indeed a 'sore plague' with which the murmurers were visited.

Prior to the miraculous destruction of Korah, Dathan and Abiram, Moses in very remarkable words gives the people a test whereby they might know that he had been sent of God 'to do all these works: [1] If these men die the common death of all men, or if they be visited after the visitation of all men, then the Lord hath not sent me. But if the Lord make a new thing, and the earth open her mouth and swallow them up, with all that appertain unto them, and they go down quick into the pit, then ye shall understand that these men have provoked the Lord.'

There appears to be here an important distinction made between the stroke by which Korah and his fellows were smitten and the subsequent 'plague' that destroyed 14,700 of the people. Yet it seems very improbable that this sudden and fearful mortality resulted from any form

[1] Numbers xvi. 28–30.

of pestilence with which we are acquainted. We are
not informed within what period of time so large a
number of people were carried off, but it would appear
to have been very brief. The command to Moses was
imperative : ' Get you up from among this congregation,
that I may consume them as in a moment ; ' and the
directions of Moses to Aaron were equally urgent:
' Take a censer, and put fire therein from off the altar,
and put on incense, and go quickly unto the congregation,
and make an atonement for them: for there is wrath
gone out from the Lord ; the plague is begun.' The
action of Aaron on receiving these instructions is
equally prompt and energetic. He ' ran into the midst
of the congregation ; and, behold, the plague was begun
among the people: and he put on incense, and made
an atonement for the people. And he stood between the
dead and the living ; and the plague was stayed.'
If this visitation was after the kind that visiteth all men,
the only forms of pestilence with which we could, as at all
likely, compare it would be either the true bubo-plague or
Asiatic cholera.   But though the Greek and Roman physicians have been supposed to have described the latter
disease, I am not aware of any evidence of cholera
having existed in Egypt in ancient times, nor indeed
have we any authentic information beyond the brief
reference which we have cited from Rufus, of the
existence of the true plague in Egypt B.C.   It is not
considered at all certain that the Athenian epidemic
during the Peloponnesian war, described by Thucydides,
was the true or bubo-plague, of which the earliest
authentic records Hirsch thinks date only from the sixth
century.[1]   From that time and through the Middle

[1] Hirsch, ch. ii. ' Plague.'

Ages it has prevailed not only as an epidemic but as a pandemic disease, its headquarters having been Egypt, Syria, and Asia Minor.

The black death of the Middle Ages, which ravaged these islands, as well as other European countries, is generally supposed to have been a form of bubo-plague characterised by special features, notably vomiting and spitting of blood and gangrenous inflammation of the lungs, rendering the breath horribly offensive and pestiferous. Other epidemiologists, however, consider the black death, or black plague, as it was sometimes called, to have been a distinct pestilence, originating in Cathay (China), and which disappeared with the fourteenth century.

The leading characteristics of true or bubo-plague may be briefly stated as a highly contagious malignant fever, attended by sudden and extreme prostration of all the powers, a leaden, sunken look of the eyes, erysipelatous inflammation of the skin, buboes, carbuncles, and petechial patches, with diarrhœa. It need scarcely be noted that we have no evidence of any such symptoms in those instances of fatal plague recorded in the Old Testament.

Small-pox is a disease of comparatively recent origin, and typhoid fever and analogous fevers, to which the wars and famines of the Dark Ages gave rise and rendered so fatal, have been the attendants of social conditions altogether different from those of the Israelites. But whilst the outbreak of all forms of epidemic pestilence may be more or less sudden in particular localities, it is only as they spread among the people of a district that any great mortality ensues, which again diminishes as the epidemic gradually subsides.

In making choice from the three forms of punishment offered to David[1] for his numbering of the people, he selected that of 'three days' pestilence,' saying, 'Let us fall now into the hand of the Lord, for His mercies are great: and let me not fall into the hand of man. So the Lord sent a pestilence upon Israel from the morning even to the time appointed: and there died of the people from Dan even to Beersheba seventy thousand men.' In the subsequent account of David's contrition and offering of his burnt-offering, this pestilence is spoken of as the plague. 'The Lord was entreated for the land, and the plague was stayed from Israel.'

Here we have an account of a pestilence which more accords with the outbreak and spread of an epidemic disease throughout the land, lasting some days, the particular nature of which it would be vain to discuss, but which may have been brought about by some sudden atmospheric change, as in certain severe outbreaks of fatal influenza.

There is nothing in the great mortality attending the scriptural instances at all unlike that which has been seen in epidemics of the bubo-plague. In the London epidemic of 1625 no less than 34,000 died, and in 1665, since which time the disease has disappeared from our country, 10,000 died; 40,000 in Marseilles in 1720, and 43,000 in Messina in 1743. In many cases death occurred within twenty-four hours, and in many more within the third to the sixth day. Such visitations have generally lasted many months, and the mortality has always been greatest at the commencement. The same may be said of Asiatic cholera. But in all the mortality has been

[1] 2 Sam. xxiv. 12.

spread over a much longer period than in the case of any of the Biblical plagues.

What interpretation we are to put on the vivid description of Zechariah,[1] of the plague with which the Lord threatens to 'smite all the people that have fought against Jerusalem,' it is very difficult to say. 'Their flesh shall consume away while they stand upon their feet, and their eyes shall consume away in their holes, and their tongue shall consume away in their mouth.' If the description be not altogether metaphorical, may it be intended to describe an army dying of famine? For the subsequent verses show that the same plague was to fall on the cattle of the enemy, as in the fifth plague of Egypt there was to be a grievous murrain of cattle.

We need not refer to various passages where moral evil is spoken of as a plague, such as 1 Kings viii. 37, 38, where 'the plague of his own heart,' which every man should know, is associated with famine, pestilence, and whatsoever plague and whatsoever sickness there may be among the people. The wicked, we are told in Ps. lxxiii, 'are not in trouble as other men, neither are they plagued like other men.'

From time immemorial the various pestilences with which nations have been visited have been looked on as Divine judgments, which they have sought to avert by sacrifices, penances, and prayers. And this acknowledgment may have been the origin of the use of the word plague, or stroke, as applicable to all and every form of destructive pestilence, and even of every special individual affliction. 'The arrow that flieth by day' is a figurative expression used by the Arabs, who speak of the pestilence as 'God's arrow, which will always hit His

---

[1] Zech. xiv. 12.

mark,' and ' What, is not the plague the dart of Almighty God, and can we escape the blow that He levels at us ? Is not His hand steady to hit the person He aims at ?'

SECTION II.—*Boils and Blains.*

The sixth plague with which Pharaoh and the people of Egypt were visited for refusing to let the Israelites depart is thus described in Exodus ix. 8, et seq. : 'And the Lord said unto Moses and unto Aaron, Take to you handfuls of ashes of the furnace, and let Moses sprinkle it toward the heaven in the sight of Pharaoh.

' And it shall become small dust in all the land of Egypt, and shall be a boil breaking forth with blains upon man, and upon beast, throughout all the land of Egypt.

' And they took ashes of the furnace, and stood before Pharaoh ; and Moses sprinkled it up toward heaven ; and it became a boil breaking forth with blains upon man, and upon beast.

' And the magicians could not stand before Moses because of the boils; for the boil was upon the magicians, and upon all the Egyptians.

' And the Lord hardened the heart of Pharaoh, and he hearkened not unto them ; as the Lord had spoken unto Moses.'

The word which our translators here render boils is by the Septuagint termed ἕλκη, elsewhere rendered sore, or ulcer, the Hebrew word being שְׁחִין. Blains in the Greek is rendered φλυκτίδες, *phlyctenæ* of medical writers, the Hebrew being אֲבַעְבֻּעֹת.

In the tenth verse the words, ' and it became a boil breaking forth with blains,' are in the Greek ἐγένετο ἕλκη

φλυκτίδες ἀναζέουσαι. These words have been by some
authorities rendered, 'they became cutaneous eruptions
accompanied by inflammation' breaking out. By
Dathe the Hebrew is rendered 'ulcera tumescentia,' and
by Rosenmuller 'inflammatio pustulas emittens.' The
same Greek word ἕλκος is used to designate Hezekiah's
disease, called boil in the A.V. This seems to be the
most appropriate rendering in the case of the plague now
under consideration ; and the Old Saxon word *blain*,
which is equivalent to bleb, or blister, is equally appropriate to express the sense of *phlyctenæ*.

Boils and *carbuncles* are analogous diseases; their
pathology is essentially the same, so far as regards the
character of the inflammation occasioning the local affection. In both it is attended by much heat and pain, and
in both leads to death or sloughing of the central parts,
constituting in the boil what is called the 'core,' and in
carbuncles to more extensive gangrene and sloughing
both of the deep-seated structures and of the skin itself,
so as to produce an extensive and deep open ulcer of
a formidable character.

Boils, however (*furunculi*), are generally a comparatively trifling disease and unattended by constitutional
disturbance. They may occur either singly, or in suc-
cession, are more frequent at certain seasons than at
others, and sometimes assume an epidemic character.
For the most part they are confined to particular regions
of the surface, though occasionally distributed over the
body. During the early stage of acute inflammation,
the point of the swelling is often occupied by a small
blister, and after the dead tissues have obtained exit
there remains, for some time, a small scar marking the
central spot.

E

A *carbuncle* is always a much more formidable disease. Anthrax and charbon (Fr.) are the nosological terms by which it is now commonly designated. The local inflammation is generally considered to have a specific character, i.e. induced by a poisoned or morbid state of the blood, and therefore associated with constitutional symptoms endangering the life of the patient. The most usual seat of the local inflammation is the back, or back of the neck, and the swelling from the first is more extended and undefined than in the case of an ordinary boil. A vesicle or vesicles arise on the prominent livid portion of the swelling, which after bursting and discharging a thin serum, reveal numerous openings, whence a purulent discharge issues for some days, till at length more or less extensive portions of dead tissue slough out, and leave a deep excavated ulcer. The scar after healing is generally more or less uneven, livid, and permanent. There is a particular carbuncular disease often called ' malignant pustule,' which requires notice for our present purpose, because it prevails among cattle and is very destructive. It is sometimes called 'splenic fever,' and, according to modern pathological views, is due to the presence in the blood of a particular microbe termed *bacillus anthracis*. Having been frequently communicated to man by the handling of wool from the diseased sheep, it is sometimes called ' wool-sorters' disease,' and in Siberia the ' Siberian plague.'

This disease, when occurring in man, so far as we at present know, is derived either from direct or indirect transmission from the lower animals, horned cattle or sheep. It appears to be endemic in certain regions, and often assumes an epidemic character. It has been investigated with remarkable skill and success by the distinguished man whose name and reputation are world-wide, M. Pasteur. Among other remarkable discoveries he has shown that this particular bacillus may be propagated in the earth around the carcases of buried infected animals, and then brought to the surface through the medium of earth worms, and thus distributed on the pasture where animals previously healthy are feeding. Treatment has hitherto proved of little value where the disease has taken possession of the system, and prevention becomes all-important. But this is surrounded by difficulties in consequence of the infecting agent being often imported from a distance by means of wool, hair, and hides. Thus, from time to time, we have outbreaks of anthrax in this and other countries that prove fearfully destructive to our cattle, and entail serious loss to the agriculturist.

We have no records of epidemic boils or carbuncles in ancient literature, that I am aware of. But since the early part of the last century there have been various accounts of such outbreaks in which boils, carbuncles, and whitlows have been intermixed. In the latter part of the eighteenth century, and since then, numerous histories have been given of Oriental boils and various sores, which have received special names from the countries in which they occurred and from other circumstances; thus we have the Aleppo boil, the Bagdad sore, and in Delhi a boil disease has been prevalent from time immemorial which is now named 'Arungzebe,' after the prince who reigned there in the eighteenth century, and who is said to have died of the boil. The so-called Aleppo boil is still prevalent, not only in Syria and Mesopotamia, but also at Suez and Cairo, as well as in Central Asia. A very general opinion obtains that in all the places where the

disease exists, it is of local endemic origin, and is introduced to the bodies of the people by the drinking water ;
facts which strongly support the theory that it is of
parasitic origin, whether the original habitat of the
parasite be in the water or the soil.

In connexion with the last observation, it is deserving
of notice that the sixth plague of boils and blains was
inflicted after the miraculous conversion of the water of
all the rivers and streams and ponds into blood, whatever
interpretation may be given of that word ; so that the
fish that was in the river died, and the river stank, and the
people loathed to drink of the water. But, apart from all
consideration of the question of parasitic organisms, it is
fair to infer that the health of the people may thus have
been so deteriorated as to render them prone to disease,
especially as the murrain of cattle followed the drinking
of the foul water, and exposed the people to the well-
known risks from the consumption of diseased meat.
Nor must we forget the nature of the other plagues that
preceded the sixth, the plagues of frogs, lice, and flies.
The health of the whole country, so far as regarded the
Egyptians, could not fail to have been seriously affected
thereby. The frogs, we are told, 'died out of the houses,
out of the villages, and out of the fields. And they
gathered them together upon heaps, and the land stank.'
Of the lice it is said, 'All the dust of the land became
lice in man and beast.' By the fourth plague, 'there
came a grievous swarm of flies into the house of Pharaoh,
and into his servants' houses, and into all the land of
Egypt ; the land was corrupted (or destroyed) by reason
of the swarm of flies.' The conclusion seems inevitable
that by such dire inflictions the whole country must have
become so insalubrious as to render the inhabitants apt

recipients of almost any disease, whilst the Israelites, shut up in the land of Goshen, were protected even from the flies that pass so easily through the air, and had no need to feed on tainted cattle. We are not told what intervals may have elapsed between the several plagues, but the consequences would be such as assuredly would not prove of short duration as regards the health of the people. Without, therefore, throwing doubt on the miraculous character of the sixth any more than of the other plagues, we are justified in concluding that the Egyptians were in such a state of deteriorated health as to render them eminently predisposed to the different forms of carbuncular disease. It is only in accordance with the action of the Divine Governor in other instances to make natural laws subservient to His special purposes, whether of mercy or judgment.

In support of the view that the boils and blains of this sixth plague may have been analogous to the *anthrax* now known as the splenic disease of cattle, it is deserving of notice that the immediately preceding plague was the murrain by which 'all the cattle of Egypt died.' On the parasitic theory, the Egyptians by contact with and eating of such cattle might become infected with the *bacillus anthracis*, or some similar microbe, and present the well-known phenomena of boils and blisters. It must, however, be observed that no mention is made of any ensuing mortality. It is merely said that the 'magicians could not stand before Moses because of the boils ; for the boil was upon the magicians, and upon all the Egyptians.'

Attempts have been made to identify this sixth plague with the small-pox. But in the first place it must be affirmed that we have no evidence whatever that the variola, or small-pox, existed in the Mosaic era. That it existed in China before it was known in Europe is generally allowed, and immemorial traditions are said to exist among the Brahmins of its existence in India, and it has been conjectured that it was from India that the disease passed both into Europe and Africa. The keenest discussions have been held as to whether the disease was known to the earliest medical writers. Rhazes in his treatise of the tenth century, *De Variolis et Morbillis*,[1] is believed to be the first medical authority who gives an unambiguous account, and who quotes fragments from an Alexandrian physician Ahron, of the date of the fifth or sixth century. But Rhazes and subsequent writers speak of the disease as generally known throughout the East. Those who, like Dr. Baron in his life of Jenner, have taken the view that small-pox was the sixth Egyptian plague, have attributed great importance to a passage from Philo the Jew, who lived in the first century, and who has given us a description of the plague of boils and blains according to his view.[2]

The passage from Philo is as follows : ' Clouds of dust being suddenly raised, and striking against both man and beast, caused ill-looking ulcers over almost the whole skin; so that immediately an efflorescent eruption made its appearance on the surface of the body, which became swollen and abounding with purulent pustules, and which you might almost think boiled in consequence of some sudden heat; but if they suffered thus much in body, they suffered more, or certainly not less, in mind, being oppressed and worn down with pain and anguish, as there appears reason, on account of the inflammation and ulceration. For to one regarding those cases, in

[1] Eng. Trans. by Greenhill. Syd. Soc. 1848.   [2] *Vita Mosis*, i. 22.

which the pustules were scattered over the body and limbs, and run together in one mass, it appeared as if they were a continual ulcer from head to foot.' Whether this passage justified Dr. Willan in saying that it contains a lively and accurate description of small-pox may be doubted. But even so, there is still more doubt whether it can be justly applied to the plague of boils and blains as described by Moses. Nor would this application receive further support, were we to attempt any more detailed description of so well-known a disease as small-pox, which could not have failed to entail so great a mortality among the people as to have demanded mention by the sacred historian.

SECTION III.—*Fevers and Inflammations.*

The Hebrew, Greek and Latin words for fever all indicate a burning heat, and it is from the Latin *febris* that our word fever has been derived. Along with this characteristic feature there are associated quickness of pulse and disturbance of function of the various organs of the body in all fevers.

Febrile disorders are among the most common diseases of the East, and have been from the earliest times. They are, however, of various kinds and of different origin. In many cases the febrile symptoms are only symptomatic of some local inflammation, though by non-professional observers they would often be called simply fever. In others the fever originates in some specific deleterious agent, introduced from without and acting as a poison on the whole system, giving rise either to a febrile state lasting continuously for a definite period, as in typhus or small-pox, or to an intermittent

febrile condition, as in common ague. To determine to
which of these kinds of fever any particular case should
be referred, would require much more detailed descriptions than are given to us in the Bible. We know,
however, that malarious diseases, which are more or less
distinctly intermittent or remittent in character, have
from the earliest times been prevalent both in Egypt
and Palestine. We know also that epidemic fevers of
a contagious kind, and spreading independent of local
causes, have from time to time prevailed, constituting
often what we have spoken of under the head of plagues.

In Deut. xxviii. 21, 22 we may perhaps discern all
these forms of fever. In verse 21 we read, 'The Lord
shall make the pestilence (θάνατος) (דֶּבֶר) cleave unto
thee, until He have consumed thee from off the land.'
(A. and R. V.) This may very probably be supposed to
denote either the true Oriental plague, or an analogous
epidemic destroying multitudes of people. The 'consumption' (ἀπορία), if it refer to disease at all, may imply
the hopeless wasting hectic fever of pulmonary and
some other diseases. 'And with a fever' (A. V.) (πυρετός)
may denote some form of continued fever; 'and with an
inflammation' (A. V.) (ῥίγει), the rigor and following heat
of intermittent malarious fever, as this is the Greek
word used by Hippocrates to denote a paroxysm of
ague. 'And with fiery heat' (R. V.) or an 'extreme
burning' (A. V.) (ἐρεθισμῷ), some of the various forms of
cutaneous inflammation, attended by heat and irritation,
such as what is called 'prickly heat.' This appears
to be the sense in which the word was employed by
Hippocrates.

In Leviticus xxvi. 16 we have again consumption
allied with 'burning ague' in A. V., and with 'fever' in

R. V., and by the LXX rendered ψώρα, a word used by medical writers to denote 'itch,' which is often attended by great heat and irritation.

The writing which the prophet Elijah sent to King Jehoram[1] says, 'Behold, with a great plague will the Lord smite thy people and thy children and thy wives and all thy goods. And thou shalt have great sickness by disease of thy bowels, until thy bowels fall out by reason of the sickness day by day.' There can be little doubt that epidemic dysentery is here denoted. The fever and inflammation of the lining membrane of the bowels which attend that disease are often of a very severe character, and marked by such discharges from the bowels as to lead the ignorant to suppose that the bowels themselves are cast out. In Jehoram's case the disease assumed a chronic form ere it ended fatally. 'And after all this the Lord smote him in his bowels with an incurable disease. And it came to pass, that in process of time, after the end of two years, his bowels fell out by reason of his sickness: so he died of sore diseases.'[2]

In Acts xxviii. 8 we have recorded the healing of the father of Publius by the apostle Paul. This man in the A. V. is said to have lain 'sick of a fever, and of a bloody flux,' and in the R. V. 'of fever and dysentery.' But St. Luke employs the plural (πυρετοῖς) in describing the fever, and doubtless does so with his usual accuracy. It is not, however, very clear what is implied by this use of the plural form. It is well known that dysentery is frequently associated with malarious intermittent fevers; it is therefore possible that the plural form was used to

---

[1] 2 Chron. xxi. 12 et seq.
[2] It would only be in accordance with medical experience if in such a case portions of the intestines had mortified and been cast out.

indicate merely the recurring paroxysms of the aguish
disease ; or it may imply that in addition to the febrile
signs of the malarious disease, the severity of the
dysentery kept up that state of fever which accompanies
all forms of inflammatory disorder, and that the patient
had thus a double form of fever, symptomatic and
essential, as they would be termed.

The words (πυρετὸs μέγαs) used by St. Luke [1] to characterise the 'great fever' of which Simon's wife's mother lay
sick, has very properly been cited as another instance in
evidence of the accuracy of language employed by the
physician when speaking of disease.   Fevers were divided
by Galen and the Greek physicians into greater and
lesser, and there can be little doubt that the disease, in
this case, was some form of continued and probably
malignant fever.   The miraculous nature of the cure is
therefore more manifest, when it is said that 'immediately she arose and ministered unto them.'   For on the
ordinary subsidence of a 'great fever' the debility and
prostration are such that many days would elapse ere the
invalid would be capable of rising to minister.

So again in the case of the nobleman's son (John
iv. 52), who was at the point of death when Jesus said
to the distressed father, 'Go thy way, thy son liveth,'
we are told that at the same hour the fever (πυρετός)
left him.   Assuming from the single word employed
to designate the disease that it was in this instance also
a continued fever rapidly passing to a fatal termination,
the sudden departure, not mere amendment of the fever,
could only have been miraculous.   The nobleman
enquired of his servants who met him the hour when
his son 'began to amend ;' and they replied, 'Yesterday at

[1] Luke iv. 38, 39.

the seventh hour the fever left him,' that being the hour at which Jesus had said, 'Thy son liveth.' The supposition that the sudden departure of the fever merely indicated the termination of a paroxysm of intermittent fever seems inconsistent with the whole tenour of the account given us.

CHAPTER III.

OPHTHALMIC DISEASES AND BLINDNESS.

THE special observances with regard to the blind that are mentioned in the Old Testament, would indicate that they were a numerous class at the time of the Exodus. 'Cursed be he that maketh the blind to wander out of the way.' In the New Testament we not only have special instances of our Lord's giving them sight, but repeated references, in general terms, to the blind as a class, who found in Jesus evidence of His Messiahship by their recovery of sight at His hands.

It is notorious that ophthalmic disease and blindness have always been very common in the East, and are so still. Egyptian ophthalmia has long been known as one of the most severe and destructive forms of inflammation of the eye. In proof of this it is only necessary to refer to the military annals, both English and French, of the Napoleonic and other Egyptian campaigns. Various causes have been assigned for its prevalence in Egypt and other Eastern climes, especially intensity of light and heat, together with searching winds filling the air with fine sand and other irritating matters, which may be sufficient to account for its wide-spreading prevalence at certain times. But the Egyptian ophthalmia is also contagious and communicable by the transfer of the purulent secretion from one eye to another. By this kind of ophthalmia the sight is often rapidly destroyed, and even the whole eye disorganised. It has sometimes spread with fearful rapidity as an epidemic through multitudes of people, leaving no small numbers permanently blind.

We cannot, however, suppose it to have been by any such form of disease that either the men of Sodom or the Syrian army, as recorded 2 Kings vi. 18, were struck blind. The infliction was doubtless miraculous in both cases, and in the latter may possibly have taken the form of temporary amaurosis, i. e. sudden paralysis or suspension of function of the optic nerve, to be after a while restored. This also may probably have been the case with St. Paul (Acts ix). The intensity of the bright light from heaven may have been sufficient to destroy the functional power of the optic nerve to a degree that would have been permanent but for its gracious restoration by the hands of Ananias. When it is said that 'immediately there fell from his eyes as it had been scales,' the language is evidently metaphorical.

We are also disposed to regard the case of Elymas as one of temporary loss of the visual function. (Acts xiii. 11.) St. Paul, addressing him, said, ' Behold, the hand of the Lord is upon thee, and thou shalt be blind, not seeing the sun for a season. And immediately there fell on him a mist (ἀχλύς) and a darkness (σκότος); and he went about seeking some to lead him by the hand.' Some have sought to explain the first word, translated ' mist,' as indicating such opacities of the cornea as frequently result from disease. But Hippocrates uses a similar term to indicate murkiness or gloom, and it would seem more natural to understand it here as describing the man's first sensations ere he became more completely dark.

The case of the two blind men who followed our Lord,[1]

---

[1] Matt. ix. 27-31.

addressing Him as 'Thou Son of David,' and crying for mercy, does not admit of any confident opinion as to the cause of their blindness. There is no ground for supposing that they were congenitally blind, but rather that they were among the many others who had long been permanently blind from disease. That they afford us a signal illustration of the power of faith in the Divine Physician cannot be doubted. When they came to Him in the house, Jesus said unto them, ' Believe ye that I am able to do this? They said unto Him, Yea, Lord. Then touched He their eyes, saying, According to your faith be it unto you. And their eyes were opened.' That touch must have had a virtue in it unknown to any surgeon oculist, or mesmerist, and unpossessed by any remedial agent.

The case of Bartimæus[1] seems altogether analogous to that of the two men just mentioned; but the blind and dumb man of Matt. xii. 22 appears to have been a case of demoniacal possession, who, when healed, both spake and saw, and gave occasion, as did Bartimæus, to the admission that the great Healer was indeed the Son of David, predicted to give sight to the blind.

Cataract is the most frequent cause of congenital blindness, and this we may with great probability assume was the nature of the case of the man blind from his birth, recorded in the ninth chapter of St. John's Gospel, who was well and publicly known to be blind. The case is remarkable, not only from the signal and miraculous nature of the cure, but also from the judicial enquiry that followed, and from the solemn and impressive discourse of our Lord to which it gave occasion, as well as to the wrath and angry discussion of the Pharisees.

[1] Luke xviii. 35–43; Mark x. 46–52.

Whether cataract, or any other form of congenital defect, was the cause of the blindness, it is impossible to suppose that it was by any inherent virtue in the subsidiary means employed, no doubt for wise reasons, by the Divine Healer, that sight was given to ' one born blind.' 'As long as I am in the world, I am the light of the world,' said Jesus. 'When He had thus spoken, He spat on the ground, and made clay of the spittle, and He anointed the eyes of the blind man with the clay, and said unto him, Go, wash in the pool of Siloam (which is by interpretation, Sent). He went his way therefore, and washed, and came seeing.' ' And it was the Sabbath day when Jesus made the clay, and opened his eyes.' Were such proceedings enjoined by our Lord with the view of rendering manifest His exercise of supernatural power and the inadequacy of the natural agents em- ployed? Or was it more signally to condemn the Pharisaic making void the law, and to show that the Son of Man was Lord of the Sabbath?

The case mentioned by St. Mark[1], where the restoration to sight was not at once complete, but by a double exercise of Divine power, seems still more distinctly to show that the cure was not due in any way to the natural external means employed. The description given by this man, when only partially in possession of sight, that ' he saw men as trees walking,' rather indicates that he had not always been blind. It was only when Christ had put ' His hands again upon his eyes, and made him look up,' that ' he was restored, and saw every man clearly.' The word 'restored' (ἀποκατεστάθη), whilst showing that sight had at one time been possessed, throws no light on the cause of the blindness. Cataract, when not strictly

[1] Mark viii. 22-26.

congenital, often occurs very early in life, at three or four years of age; and had this been the case here the man might have retained some knowledge of sight. But it is more probable that sight had been lost by some of those forms of inflammation or other ophthalmic disease which were common, and had occurred at a more advanced age. In either case, had the cure been by ordinary means, sight would not have returned immediately, but gradually. Had the case been one of cataract of the congenital kind, some time would have been needed to admit of the man's learning to judge both of form and distance. In Chesleden's well-known case of a child on whom he operated at the age of 14, and who had been blind from birth, the lad at first had no judgment of distance, or the shape of things, whatever might be their size or form, and only gradually acquired a knowledge of things by sight alone, requiring for some time to aid his judgment by the sense of touch.

The blind of our day have reason to be thankful for the efforts that are made to enable them to come to the knowledge of Him who is 'the light of the world,' though deprived of the ordinary means of becoming acquainted with His revealed truth. It is said that in Cairo there are now thousands of blind, and that in the island of Formosa they amount to seven or eight thousand. For the blind in Formosa there has recently been produced a Chinese primer in raised type, to enable them, as well as those in our own land, to read the Scriptures in their native tongue, and thus to look on Him who, not only still gives sight to the blind, but also teaches His disciples to be imitators of Himself.

CHAPTER IV.

DISEASES OF THE NERVOUS SYSTEM.

SECTION I.—*Lunacy and Demoniacal Possession.*

ALTHOUGH it is beyond the scope of this little volume to discuss the subject of Biblical psychology, a few remarks from a medical point of view are called for on some of the cases recorded, both in the Old and New Testaments, which would fall under this head. Science has not yet been able to solve the mystery of the natural and normal relation of mind to matter by which our daily life is characterised and influenced. Still less is it competent to deal with what we are compelled to call the supernatural. That lunacy is in a large proportion of cases associated with recognisable material changes in the brain, and often the direct result of cerebral disease, cannot be questioned. But that perverted or dethroned reason may not in other cases be the direct result of Divine interposition science is not in a position to deny. Nor can those who receive the Bible in any true sense as a Divine revelation doubt that it teaches the existence of angelic beings, both good and evil, who are commissioned or permitted to exercise powers that we can only call supernatural. Theologians may be unable to account for the origin of evil, or to tell us how and to what extent the 'principalities and powers and the rulers of the darkness of this world' can exercise their evil

F

agency, but they cannot deny either the existence of such agents or that they are permitted in some way or other to take part in the Divine government. There is a kingdom of Satan, though subservient to the kingdom of God.

Whether there be in the present day such a thing as demoniacal possession, in the sense in which it was understood in the time of our Lord, we are not called upon to enquire; although it may be admitted that there is not a little in the manifestations of many cases of lunacy that may well give rise to the question whether Satanic agency has not some part therein. Religious men of the most irreproachable character, and women of unsullied purity of thought and habit, will use language, entertain ideas and manifest conduct altogether opposed to their character in a sane state, and which become the source of the utmost pain and distress of mind when restored to reason. But such cases, or even certain specific forms of insanity which have been designated by such terms as ' theomania ' and ' caco-demonomania,' afford little or no help towards an explanation of many of the instances of possession by devils recorded in the New Testament. Nor does it appear to us possible, on any principles of medical science, to refer these to any known form of bodily disease. In several passages in the Gospels they are distinctly separated from ordinary diseases, and especially by St. Luke, the physician, when recording the interview between John's disciples and our Lord, 'In that hour He cured many of diseases and plagues and evil spirits.'[1] In Matt. iv. 24 we have not only diseases in general, but also lunacy, specifically distinguished from ' divers diseases and torments.' But our Lord's

[1] Luke vii. 21. (R.V.)

own language is decisive of the question.   He commands
the unclean spirit to come out of a man—speaks of
'casting out devils'—suffers others to enter into a
herd of swine—of 'the unclean spirit, when he is
gone out of a man, walking through dry places,' of
'taking to himself seven other spirits more wicked
than himself;' in this last instance clearly denoting, not
any particular disease, but 'spirits' in the plural number.
Language such as this it seems impossible to interpret in
a figurative or popular sense.   Doubtless many of the
demoniacs may truly be said to have been insane, and
in one instance he is called 'lunatic,'[1] and manifested
epileptic symptoms similar to what are seen in epileptic
maniacs of the present day.   In another instance, after
being cured, the man is said to be 'sitting clothed, and
in his right mind.'   But the whole subject of demoniacal
possession we do not attempt to discuss.

SECTION II.—*Saul's Disease.*

There is not a more melancholy history recorded in
the Bible than that of the first King of Israel, nor anywhere a more striking dramatic contrast of character
than that afforded by Saul and his successor David.

When they were first introduced to each other,[2] Saul
must have been considerably past middle age, and, even
if unacquainted with the anointing and designation of
David, had been told that his kingdom had been rent
from him and 'given to another better than he.'   He
knew that he was rejected of God, deserted by his faithful
friend the prophet, and that his authority was discredited.
His pride was deeply wounded, he was conscious of a

---

[1] Matt. xvii. 15, σεληνιάζεται.   See note at the end of the volume.
[2] 1 Sam. xvi. 14 et seq.

wilful rebellious spirit, was the subject of bitter remorse
on account of his transgressions, harassed by wars and
troubles of state, wearied in body and agonised in mind.
'The Spirit of the Lord departed from Saul, and an evil
spirit from the Lord troubled (terrified) him.'

David was a happy youth, of buoyant poetic tempera-
ment, 'ruddy, and withal of a beautiful countenance,
and goodly to look to,' upon whom, after his anointing,
'the Spirit of the Lord came from that day forward.'

> 'God's child, with the dew
> On thy gracious gold hair.'[1]

There is great difficulty in reconciling the account given
in the sixteenth chapter, of the interview between the
aged monarch and the stripling shepherd, with that
recorded in the following chapter, which took place after
David's victory over Goliath. Both have the appearance of being the description of a first interview.
Perhaps the most probable, but by no means satisfactory
solution, is to suppose that the king had, on the second
occasion, through mental infirmity, forgotten the name
and aspect of the youthful victor, so as to make it needful
for him to ask, 'Whose son art thou, thou young man?'
But Abner also, who must have known that David had
for some time stood before the king, seems to have been
equally ignorant, and had to be told to enquire.

The question, however, for us is, What was the nature
of the king's distemper when his 'servants said unto
him, Behold now, an evil spirit from God troubleth thee.
Let our lord now command thy servants which are
before thee to seek out a man who is a cunning player
on an harp ; and it shall come to pass when the evil
spirit from God is upon thee, that he shall play with his

[1] Browning's *Saul*.

hand, and thou shalt be well.' To this Saul assented
and 'one of the servants said, Behold, I have seen a son
of Jesse the Bethlehemite, that is cunning in playing,
and a mighty valiant man, and a man of war, and
prudent in matters, and a comely person, and the Lord
is with him ;' whereupon the son of Jesse, being sent for,
'came to Saul and stood before him : and he loved him
greatly ; and he became his armour-bearer.'

Were these servants of Saul his physicians, and if so,
what did they mean by 'an evil spirit from God?' Did
they mean to imply that their master was the subject of
demoniacal possession? But why should an evil spirit
from the Lord any more imply supernatural agency than
the 'Spirit of the Lord' which departed from Saul, or
the 'Spirit of the Lord' which came upon David from
the day of his unction? Josephus, by using the term
δαιμόνια in connexion with Saul's case, seems to indicate
that he looked on it as demoniacal possession ; and it
is quite possible that Saul's servants may have taken
the same view. But the words of the sacred writer do
not necessarily imply more than that Saul was given up
to suffer the natural consequences of his own rebellious
spirit and evil mind, which, preying on itself, terminated
in mental derangement. If this be the correct view, it
would none the less deserve to be considered as a puni-
tive dispensation from God. That the disorder was not
in the ordinary acceptation of the term supernatural may
be inferred, both from the subsequent history and from
the nature and success of the treatment adopted. This
was exactly what would now be held to be the most
appropriate and sensible in that form of mental derangement usually designated as melancholia.

That this was the form of Saul's mental disorder there

can be little doubt, and such opinion has been very generally adopted. It is a very common form of insanity, and is characterised by great mental depression, in which the patient feels his whole existence overwhelmed by gloom and anxious forebodings. It is chiefly seen in the aged or in those past middle age, rarely in young persons. Though not always to be attributed to assignable moral causes, it frequently supervenes on grief, losses and disappointments, worry and anxiety. In many instances the bodily health for a time may not seem to be much impaired, but in pronounced cases sooner or later is seriously deranged. The mental depression may pass off gradually or suddenly, to recur, or not, at uncertain intervals, from various causes. If the malady grows worse, delusions of various kinds supervene, or the case may take on some other type of insanity marked by excitement. The most common delusions are such as have a religious character, often giving rise to an unfounded belief that religion is the cause of the insanity. The patient imagines that he is the subject of some loathsome or incurable disease, that his affairs and prospects are ruined, that he has committed the unpardonable sin, that he is the object of Divine vengeance, that he is eternally lost, body and soul, and that life is no longer endurable. But even in the milder forms and early stages of the distemper the tendency to commit suicide is so common and persistent as to demand the most strict and unintermitting watching of the sufferer by night, as well as by day. A large proportion of the cases of suicide publicly recorded are from this kind of mental disorder. This is the more lamentable because they might often have been prevented, and because this form of insanity is more amenable to treatment than many others, a large proportion of cases being cured, though the disorder is apt to recur under the influence of any depressing cause, whether moral or physical.

It is not necessary to assume, nor, indeed, does it seem probable, that much of the cruel and tyrannical conduct that marked the latter part of Saul's career resulted from actual insanity, though it must be remembered that he had frequent fits of melancholic depression, and ultimately ended his life by suicide. David's success and growing popularity made him an object of jealousy and suspicion to Saul, who became afraid of him, plotted against him, laid snares for him, and more than once attempted his life. But the open way in which he spake of David, and gave orders that he should be slain, and especially the way in which he met Jonathan's remonstrance and intercession, and his capacity for appreciating the noble conduct of David, are at all events inconsistent with the view that he was continuously insane. The homicidal attacks on David when playing before him 'with his hand, as at other times,' are not, indeed, such as very often characterise melancholia, but they are occasionally seen, for, as we have said, that form of mental disorder is apt to assume another type. Such homicidal outbursts are not therefore inconsistent with the whole of the later portion of Saul's history.

Change of scene and occupation and the society of cheerful and judicious companions are the most efficacious and all-important means in the treatment of melancholia and in 'ministering to a mind diseased.' From time immemorial the soothing influence of music has been acknowledged and employed in cases like Saul's. As such it was recommended by his servants or physicians, and proved on the first, as well as on subsequent occasions, to be efficacious. Moreover we are told that from the first, when David stood before Saul, that 'he loved him greatly.' The musician therefore was evidently a *persona grata* at such time, which would be all-important to the efficacy of the remedy employed. The harpist was also a valiant youth, not to be disconcerted by angry looks or outbreaks of temper, 'prudent in matters,' and knew that 'the Lord was with him,' to direct and aid him when seeking to afford the desired relief.

Thus when the sweet singer took up his harp and played with his hand, 'Saul was refreshed, and was well, and the evil spirit departed from him.' What the music was, or what the psalms that were sung, we know not. Was it an impromptu of the twenty-third psalm to

'The tune all our sheep know, as one after one
So docile they come to the pen-door, till folding be done'[1]

with which the musician sought to soothe the monarch's troubled spirit? Or what other psalm and strain did he choose—

'Ay, to save and redeem and restore him . . .
Saul, the failure, the ruin he seems now . . .!'[2]

SECTION III.—*Nebuchadnezzar's Disease.*

As King Nebuchadnezzar walked in the palace of the kingdom of Babylon, he spake, and said, ' Is not this great Babylon, that I have built for the house of the kingdom by the might of my power, and for the honour of my majesty? While the word was in the king's mouth, there fell a voice from heaven, saying, O king Nebuchadnezzar, to thee it is spoken; The kingdom is departed from thee. And they shall drive thee from men, and thy dwelling shall be with the beasts of the field : they shall make thee to eat grass

[1] Browning's *Saul*.   [2] *Idem.*

as oxen, and seven times shall pass over thee, until thou know that the Most High ruleth in the kingdom of men, and giveth it to whomsoever He will.. The same hour was the thing fulfilled upon Nebuchadnezzar: and he was driven from men, and did eat grass as oxen, and his body was wet with the dew of heaven, till his hairs were grown like eagles' feathers, and his nails like birds'claws.'[1]

Various symbolical and fanciful interpretations have been offered of this remarkable judgment that befell the great King of Babylon. By some it has been supposed that he underwent an actual metamorphosis of body and soul. Jewish rabbins have asserted that his soul by transmigration entered into the body of an ox; others, believing the fables of the fifteenth century, of men transformed into wolves, have concluded that the king's case was an analogous instance. These and similar views are, however, clearly untenable. That the king became insane there can be no doubt, and that his insanity was characterised by wild violence, so as to render him dangerous to society and make it necessary to expel him, may be inferred from the words of the judgment, 'they shall drive thee from men, and thy dwelling shall be with the beasts of the field.' It is not distinctly stated that he was the subject of any specific delusion; but we can have little doubt that the opinion most commonly entertained is correct, and that his insanity was attended by that kind of delusion which led him to fancy that he was changed into an ox. Similar insane delusions are not infrequently met with.

There is much in the history of this monarch that would warrant the supposition that his mental derangement was the result of his unbridled passions, his pride,

[1] Daniel iv. 29 et seq.

ambition, worldly success and exaltation. In certain
forms of insanity the earliest indications are exaggerated
and false notions of the individual's importance and
position in life, together with a general exaltation of
views. But whatever may have been the influence of
such predisposing causes as may be admitted to have
existed, we cannot read the whole history without seeing
that the ultimate dethronement of reason was a part of the
judgment predicted, and that it was attended by features
that must have been peculiarly humiliating and degrading
to a grand and mighty king. This was acknowledged by
the king himself in the public proclamation that he
caused to be sent to all his subjects, and in the confession
that he makes when restored: 'Now I Nebuchadnezzar
praise and extol and honour the King of Heaven, all
whose works are truth, and His ways judgment: and *those
that walk in pride He is able to abase.*'

Among the various delusions of the insane, none are
more common than those which relate to their bodily
sensations and condition. Modifications in the sensation
of self are not infrequently met with, and lead to the idea
of personal transformation. Former personality may be
ignored and patients imagine themselves lords, dukes, and
kings, or animals, cocks, wolves, dogs, or oxen, whilst at
the same time their real personality is retained. Sometimes they fancy the material structure of their body to be
changed, and to have become wood or glass. Thus in
what has been termed 'lycanthropia,' the ' wehr wolf' of
the Germans, the delusion consists in the belief that the
patient has become a wolf. Cases of this kind are said
to have occurred in Alsatia in the fifteenth century, the
patients running about on all fours, howling and attacking
children ; and there are others mentioned in the classics

analogous to that of the King of Babylon. Virgil tells us that the daughters of Prœtus, believing themselves to be cows, ran into the fields and

'Implerunt falsis mugitibus agros,'[1]

If by 'seven times' we are to understand seven years that the king was exiled from human society, there is not much difficulty in understanding other features of his câse. When it is said, 'Let a beast's heart be given unto him,' let him be deprived of reason and believe himself an ox is probably all that is meant. Eating grass like an ox does not necessarily imply that he had no other food. Driven from men, and the object of dread and aversion, he may still have been an object of compassion, or may have been able to obtain fruits or grain. But eating grass and all kinds of garbage is not uncommon with the insane. From long neglect and exposure to the dews of heaven, it is not surprising that his hair should have 'grown like eagles' feathers and his nails as birds' claws.' When long uncut and neglected, and after much exposure to the weather, the hair becomes coarse and more or less matted, so as to resemble feathers; and in like manner the nails, if not pared, will attain to a length of 1½ or even 2 inches, and curve round the ends of the fingers and toes, as may often be seen in many of the Chinese, and thus resemble a bird's claws.

It has been objected that such insanity as that of Nebuchadnezzar would have rendered him incapable of praying. It is, however, well known that many of the insane will attend public worship, and practise private prayer, as before their loss of reason. It would, however, rather seem that it was only after his restoration that the king is represented to have prayed.

[1] Eclog. vi. 48.

That his reason had been dethroned the king was quite aware when 'at the end of the days,' he says, 'I lifted up mine eyes unto heaven, and mine under- standing returned unto me, and I blessed the Most High, and I praised and honoured Him that liveth for ever.' 'He doeth according to His will in the army of heaven, and among the inhabitants of the earth, and none can stay His hand, or say unto Him, What doest Thou?' Thus the first use that he made of his restored reason was to acknowledge the justice of the Almighty Ruler of men, and offer a song of praise for the mercy vouch- safed him.

SECTION IV.—*Paralysis and Palsy.*

These terms, if not absolutely synonymous, are often used interchangeably. Palsy is popularly used to denote a loss of *motor* power in a muscle or set of muscles, and is then equivalent to *motor paralysis.* In this sense it seems to be employed in the Authorised Version of the New Testament. Where there is loss of power to transmit *sensory* impressions to the brain, it would be called *sensory paralysis.* If we restrict both terms to the loss of motor power, we shall find that this may depend on disease of the brain, spinal cord, or particular nerves, and that this may result from simple mechanical injury or morbid changes, whether local or general, in- volving the system at large, and manifested through the nervous system. In some cases the paralysis depends on temporary causes capable of removal, in others, and more frequently, on such alteration of structure as involves permanent loss of function. These latter are by far the most common, and therefore ordinarily a person who is said to be palsied is permanently disabled in some way. Two of the most common forms are when either one side of the body is affected (*hemiplegia*) or the lower limbs (*paraplegia*).

In the latter case, when pronounced, all locomotion is prevented; and if, as sometimes happens, the arms are also paralysed, these also would be useless, and the subject unable to help himself in any way.

It seems probable that this last most serious and hopeless form of disease characterised the case of 'one sick of the palsy' who was borne of four and brought to our Lord for healing at Capernaum.[1] That it was no slight form of disease, which might only in popular language be called palsy, is shown by the special term (παραλελυμένος) employed by the Evangelist Luke, as this is the correct technical Greek word for pronounced paralysis from disease of some part of the nervous system. That the subject was an adult we infer from four men being required to carry him, and that he was young, Bengel thinks, is implied by the word son (τέκνον) used by our Lord when first addressing him, saying, ' Thy sins be forgiven thee.' But is it therefore necessary to assume that his disease was the direct result of any special sin, or of an immoral life, any more than in the case of the impotent man at the pool of Bethesda, who was enjoined to 'sin no more, lest a worse thing come unto thee?'

But whatever may have been the nature of the cause by which this complete loss of power was brought about, it was evidently such as no known means of medical treatment could have effected the cure of instantaneously, if at all. The miraculous character of the cure is evident not only from the rapidity with which it was effected,

[1] Matt. ix; Mark ii; Luke v.

but also from the evidence we have that muscular power of robust health was so completely gained as to enable the man not merely to raise himself up and walk, but also to carry a load. This would have been impossible in any known form of long-standing paralysis, even had it been functional only, as in what is called hysterical paralysis, in which, however, there is never that complete loss of all power here indicated, and where it is mainly the will that is at fault.

Similar evidence of the miraculous nature of the cure is afforded by the case of Æneas, recorded in Acts ix. 33, who 'had kept his bed eight years, and was sick of the palsy,' when Peter said to him, ' Æneas, Jesus Christ maketh thee whole : arise, and make thy bed. And he arose immediately.' No satisfactory explanation of such cures can be given by medical or any natural science. If the authenticity of the facts be admitted, we are compelled to refer them to the category of the super-natural.

In the centurion's servant who, according to St. Matthew,[1] lay 'at home sick of the palsy (paralytic), *grievously tormented*,' and whom St. Luke describes[2] as 'sick and ready to die,' we have probably a case of progressive paralysis, attended by muscular spasms and involving the respiratory movements, where death is manifestly imminent and inevitable. Such a case would be attended by symptoms indicative of great distress as well as immediate danger to life.

The impotent man at the pool of Bethesda,[3] one of the 'great multitude of impotent (sick) folk, of blind, halt, withered, waiting for the moving of the water,' has also been thought to have been the subject of palsy;

---

[1] Matt. viii. 6.   [2] Luke vii. 2.   [3] John v. 2-9.

but of this there is much reason to doubt. He is said to have 'had an infirmity thirty-and-eight years;' but that this did not incapacitate him for all movement is shown by his own words, 'while I am coming another steppeth down before me.' Among the 'halt and withered' there would very probably be cases of chronic rheumatism and joint disease and other wasting (withering) diseases, which would be likely to benefit by the waters, whatever opinion may be entertained of the authenticity of verse 4. For such diseases, as well as for various forms of nervous affections, baths were anciently in repute, and the words ' of whatsoever disease he had ' seem to imply that the waters were had recourse to for various maladies. There does not, therefore, appear sufficient evidence to enable us to say confidently that this man's disease was either *locomotor ataxy* or other chronic hopeless nervous disease, or indeed what it was. But the miraculous character of the cure is sufficiently shown by the fact that the man was made at once so 'perfectly whole' as to be able to take up his bed and walk.[1]

The case described by St. Luke xiii. 11–17 of 'a woman which had a spirit of infirmity eighteen years, and was bowed together, and could in no wise lift up herself,' I cannot consider, as some have done, to have been a case of paralysis strictly so called. For in the first place, though recorded by the Evangelist Luke alone, he does not call it palsy, which he pretty certainly would have done, as in the case at Capernaum, had it been such. The woman's condition is very characteristically described as bowed down and quite unable to lift

---

[1] Some have maintained that this man was an impostor whose feigned disease our Lord exposed.

up herself, although in the synagogue among the other attendants. 'And when Jesus saw her, He *called her to Him* and said unto her, Woman, thou art loosed from thine infirmity. And He laid His hands on her : and immediately she was *made straight.*' Her case seems in all probability to have been such an one as is not unfrequently met with in the present day, even in the streets, in which there is a gradual wasting and relaxation of the muscles and ligaments of the back, by which the trunk is held erect, so that the body falls forward, without there being any disease either of the brain or spinal cord or any mental impairment. Such cases are chiefly met with in the aged, and are progressive and permanent in character, admitting of very little relief by medical science. We are not called to offer any opinion as to the import of our Lord's words, 'whom Satan hath bound.' The case, however, does not appear to have been what would be called demoniacal possession, and the words 'loosed from this bond' appear specially appropriate to the view that we have taken of her 'infirmity.'

Various opinions have been entertained as to the nature of the case of the man 'whose right hand was withered.'[1] Withered or blighted limbs are often met with in the present day. One of the more common forms is that which is frequently called *infantile paralysis*, the result of disease in early life, occasioning arrest of development of a particular limb, without other permanent bad result, but which leaves the limb shrunk and withered. There are similar cases which are congenital. In other cases a like result follows direct injury to the main nerve of a limb, the further development and nutrition of which are impeded, and the limb

---

[1] Matt. xii. 9–13 ; Mark iii. 1–5 ; Luke vi. 6–11.

becomes wasted or withered. To any of these forms of withering may the case recorded by the three evangelists be referred. There is also a form of disease termed *dropped hand*, to which painters and others working in lead are liable, as the result of lead poisoning. Although some of the milder of such cases recover, others permanently disable the patient. To such cases, however, the term withered is not strictly applicable, nor do we think that they offer any satisfactory explanation of the case in question.

We hear much in the present day of faith healing, of cures wrought by relics or at the shrines of saints, by pretended agencies and imaginary forces, mesmeric, odylic or other, by healing virtue emanating from particular persons to other people, all of which, in various ways, demonstrate the marvellous influence exerted by mind on body. Without questioning the power of that kind of faith that can remove mountains, there can be no doubt that a large proportion of reputed faith-cures are fallacious, and will not stand the scrutiny of competent investigation. But no thoughtful and experienced physician can doubt that through mental influence of some kind, not only are the normal functions of the body, but also diseased actions, controlled, and sometimes even life preserved. Such influence is most frequently seen in connexion with mental and nervous diseases of a functional character, though sometimes of long standing and to ordinary observers of a serious and irremediable nature. 'It is therefore quite conceivable,' as Bishop Temple has observed,[1] 'that many of our Lord's miracles of healing may have been the result of this power of mind

[1] *Bampton Lectures.* Relations of Religion and Science, pp. 199 et seq.

over body.' ' It is possible that they may have been due not to an interference with the uniformity of nature, but to a superiority in His mental power to the similar power possessed by other men.' That there is considerable difference in the power which different men possess in controlling the actions of their own bodies, in enduring pain, in resisting depressing and exhausting influences and even the progress of disease, there can be no question; nor that there is a similar difference in the degree of mental power which different men can exert over the bodies of other men. But even if we should suppose that the cures of disease by our Lord were thus wrought, they would be scarcely less miraculous. For His miracles of healing were wrought on forms of disease and in ways that do not admit of explanation by any such exercise of mental power as we possess. The power that could arrest disease of a mortal character and recall to life by a word spoken at a distance, and that could raise the dead to life, was a spiritual force of a different order from that possessed by any mesmerist, magician, or mortal man.

CHAPTER V.

DISEASES OF JOB, HEROD, HEZEKIAH, JEROBOAM, AND THE SHUNAMMITE WOMAN'S SON.

I. *Job's Disease.*—This is described in Job ii. 4 et seq.: 'And Satan answered the Lord and said, Skin for skin, yea all that a man hath will he give for his life. But put forth Thine hand now, and touch his bone and his flesh, and he will curse Thee to Thy face. And the Lord said unto Satan, Behold, he is in thine hand; but save his life. So went Satan forth from the presence of the Lord, and smote Job with sore boils from the sole of his foot unto his crown. And he took him a potsherd to scrape himself withal; and he sat down among the ashes.'

The terms here employed to describe Job's sore affliction are evidently not such as to admit of our forming any very confident opinion as to what the nature of his disease was. But they are sufficient, along with the subsequent history, to show that it entailed great suffering and demands on his constancy of endurance and submission. But whilst his physical condition was such as to grievously impair his bodily health, his mental powers were retained. A very general belief has obtained that his disease was the true leprosy, the *elephantiasis Græcorum.* This opinion dates as far back as Origen, when it was said that Job was afflicted ἀγρίῳ ἐλέφαντι, τῷ οὕτω καλουμένῳ νοσήματι.[1] The Hebrew שְׁחִין, which

---

[1] *Contra Celsum*, book vi. chap. 43.

G 2

the LXX translate ἔλκος, admits of being rendered 'sore' or 'burning sore,' the radical meaning only implying burning or inflammation, the hot sense of pain which accompanies various forms of cutaneous disease.

The same Hebrew word occurs in Deut. xxviii. 35, and in various other places in the Old Testament, and is always rendered by the LXX by the same Greek word; but our translators use the term 'botch' in Deut. xxviii, 'The Lord shall smite thee in the knees and in the legs with a sore botch that cannot be healed, from the sole of thy foot unto the top of thy head.' Johnson describes 'botch' as 'a swelling or eruptive discoloration of the skin.' It can scarcely be said to be a medical term, and when used by Milton seems to be synonymous with patch, 'botches and blains must all his flesh emboss.' As derived from the Italian *bozza*, it would imply either a swelling or a rough unfinished piece of sculpture or painting. If this is what our translators meant when using the word, it might be held as an appropriate description of some of the cutaneous signs of elephantiasis. They do not, however, thus translate the same Greek word ἔλκος when speaking of Job's disease, but render ἔλκει πονηρῷ 'sore boils.' Their reason for this is not apparent, but whatever may be meant by the Hebrew שְׁחִין here, or by the words 'from the sole of his foot unto his crown,' it seems almost impossible to believe that the eruption on the skin was either what we should call ulcers or boils, when it is said that Job sat down among the ashes and used a potsherd to scrape himself with. A potsherd might be used to remove incrustations of dried matter, or to relieve the intolerable irritation and itching of various inflamed or scaly eruptions. For the latter purpose the natives of

the South Sea Islands are known to use, in the present
day, a bivalve shell. But there are other features of
Job's lamentable state deserving of notice, such as the
emaciation (xvi. 8), nights sleepless, and scared with
frightful dreams (vii. 14), 'Thou scarest me with dreams,
and terrifiest me through visions.' These are characteristic symptoms in true leprosy, and so also is the loathing
of life: 'So that my soul chooseth strangling, and death
rather than my life. I loathe it; I would not live
alway.' The words too of Satan demand special notice,
'Put forth Thine hand now, and touch his *bone* and his
flesh,' as indicating the deep-seated nature of the disease.
So also we read that on the approach of his friends,
'When they lifted up their eyes afar off, and knew him
not, they lifted up their voice and wept; and they rent
every one his mantle, and sprinkled dust upon their
heads toward heaven.' This leads us to infer that his
disfigurement was such as to make him not only un-
recognisable by his friends, but also to appal them,
which, as we have seen when speaking of elephantiasis, is
a not unfrequent effect of that terrible disease.

There is considerable difference of opinion both as to
the age of the Book of Job and his residence. If, however, he lived after the Israelites had entered the Promised
Land, we should certainly have expected his disease to
have been differently described, had it been the so-called
Levitical leprosy, and thus are afforded an additional
argument against that disease being elephantiasis, if
such was Job's disease. There are, however, other views
that have been taken of Job's malady. Burns, in his
account of Bokhara, where the guinea-worm disease
exists, says that it is there spoken of by the inhabitants
as 'the disease of Job.' Of that very remarkable and

grave parasitic disease we propose to speak under the head of Fiery Serpents. But we must own that we cannot see any analogy between it and the patriarch's disease. It has also been suggested that his malady may have been that peculiar Oriental sore known as the '*Aleppo or Bagdad evil.*'

That Job's disease was indeed a sore and loathsome one is evident, and we are perhaps justified in assuming that it was altogether of an exceptional character. We are told nothing of its removal, and its invasion is related in connexion with difficult and mysterious subjects, into which it is not our duty to enter. The antiquity and purport of the book, on which there is so much difference of opinion, and the metaphorical character of much of the writing, all render it extremely difficult to speak with confidence on the precise nature of the disease, which constituted so much of the patriarch's suffering and trial.

II. *The Disease of Herod Agrippa I.*—This able but unprincipled man, history informs us, had led a licentious and extravagant life, and it was on the occasion of a great festival, when surrounded by his grandees, that the occurrences described in Acts xii. 21–23 took place. ' Upon a set day Herod, arrayed in royal apparel, sat upon his throne, and made an oration unto them. And the people gave a shout, saying, It is the voice of a god, and not of a man. And immediately the angel of the Lord smote him, because he gave not God the glory: and he was eaten of worms, and gave up the ghost.' Josephus,[1] in recording the same event, does not mention worms as the cause of death, but says what helps us materially in deciding the nature of the disease, for he states that the king was suddenly seized,

[1] *Antiq. Jud.* xix. c. viii. sec. 2.

and, after suffering severe and tormenting pains in the
bowels, in five days died.   The two accounts considered
together leave scarcely any room for doubt that the
cause of death was perforation of the bowels by intestinal
worms, inducing ulceration and acute peritonitis. Medical
records contain such cases, and the condition of the
stomach and bowels after indulgence at a feast would
favour the occurrence of the fatal termination at such a
time.   Any abnormal distension of the bowels, especially
if associated with bodily exertion, would be sufficient to
account for rupture of the intestines at spots previously
eroded and thinned by ulcerative disease.   And there is
scarcely any suffering more severe than that which
attends peritoneal inflammation thus induced.   The term
used by Luke the physician to describe the disease
leaves no doubt, I think, that it was occasioned by worms
(σκωληκόβρωτος), and that there is no foundation for the
notion that it was what the Greeks call phthiriasis, *morbus
pedicularis*.   In other parts of Scripture σκώληξ is the
word used to denote worms, as in Exod. xvi. 20, their
manna bred worms and stank ; in Deut. xxviii. 39, of the
grapes, 'the worms shall eat them ;' Job vii. 5, ' My flesh is
clothed with worms and clods of dust.' Herodotus[1] speaks
of the mother of Arcesilaus being destroyed alive by
worms, possibly in the same way as Herod was ; but he
uses another word, εὐλή, which, however, also means
worm or maggot, such as are bred in decaying flesh, and
not the word whence the Greek term for *morbus pedicularis* is derived, which means ' louse.'

The account which Josephus gives of this most impressive narrative, as quoted by Bengel, is so graphic
that we venture to give it in full.   'Clad in a garment

[1] *Hist.* iv. 205.

which was all woven of silver, by marvellous workmanship, and which, struck by the rays of the rising sun, and emitting a kind of divine splendour, was inspiring the spectators with veneration, accompanied with awe ; and presently, after baneful flatterers raising acclamations, each from a different quarter, were hailing him as a god, begging him that he would be favourably propitious ; for that heretofore having revered him as a man, they now perceive and acknowledge that there is in him something more excellent than mortal nature ; this impious adulation he did not correct or repel. There ensued torturing pains in the belly, which were violent from the very first. Having therefore turned his eyes towards his friends, " Behold !" said he, " I, the god as you called me, am commanded to leave life, the fatal necessity of death confuting your lie ; and I, whom you hailed as immortal, am hurried away by a mortal stroke." Then, worn out by the torture, which did not at all abate for five days continuously, he ended life.'[1] He had been struck by the angel of the Lord. Was it the same angel that had released from prison the victim of his cruelty, the apostle whom he had imprisoned to please his flatterers?

III. *Hezekiah's Disease.*—But little can be said of the nature and cure of the disease with which King Hezekiah was afflicted. In all three references to his case he is said to have been sick unto death.[2] And it is therefore clear from such repeated statements, as well as from his own words in his song of praise on recovering his health, that his life had been in danger, and that it was no trifling ailment from which he had suffered. But the only distinct statement as to its nature is that given us

[1] Bengel's *Gnomon.*, Eng. Trans., vol. ii. p. 616.
[2] 2 Kings xx. 1 ; 2 Chron. xxxii. 24 ; Isaiah xxxviii. 1.

by the prophet Isaiah, who said, 'Let them take a lump of figs, and lay it for a plaister upon the *boil*, and he shall recover.'[1] When the prophet first came to him he addressed him in words clearly indicating the gravity of the disease. 'Thus saith the Lord, Set thine house in order: for thou shalt die, and not live.' We cannot therefore think that it was an ordinary simple boil with which the king was affected. Nor have we any ground for supposing, as some have suggested, that the disease was bubo-plague, which does not occur as an isolated case, and we have no evidence to lead us to think that any epidemic of such a disease prevailed. But it might have been, and probably was, a *carbuncle*, which is often a most severe and painful thing, endangering and often terminating the life of the sufferer. For this a poultice of figs would be an appropriate local remedy, as in the present day are cataplasms of various kinds. But doubtless the recovery of the king was through Divine interposition, by which the danger to life was averted, and of which Isaiah's prescription was but a symbol. The sign that was given to the king, by the going back of the shadow 'on the sundial of Ahaz,' has hitherto not been found capable of interpretation except as a miracle. The answer to his prayer, accompanied by the promise that on the *third* day he should go up to the house of the Lord, is sufficient evidence that the cure of a disease by which he had been brought to death's door was not brought about by natural means.[2]

IV. *Jeroboam's Disease.*— This, generally viewed as paralysis, may possibly have arisen from what is called 'embolism,' i.e. the blocking of an artery by

[1] Isaiah xxxviii. 21.
[2] See further on this subject Notes at the end of the volume.

a clot occurring suddenly and thus occasioning paralysis. 'And it came to pass, when King Jeroboam
heard the saying of the man of God, which had cried
against the altar in Bethel, that he put forth his
hand from the altar, saying, Lay hold on him. And
his hand, which he put forth against him, dried up, so
that he could not pull it in again to him. The altar
also was rent, and the ashes poured out from the altar,
according to the sign which the man of God had given
by the word of the Lord. And the king answered and
said unto the man of God, Intreat now the face of the
Lord thy God, and pray for me, that my hand may be
restored me again. And the man of God besought the
Lord, and the king's hand was restored him again, and
became as it was before.'[1] The king's manifest mental
excitement and terror at the time would lend support to
this view. It is, however, said not only that he could not
'pull in again' his arm, but also that it was 'dried up.'
This is unlike anything that immediately ensues on
simple embolism, but might after a while result from
muscular wasting following on embolism.

V. *Disease of the Shunammite Woman's Son.*—'And
when the child was grown, it fell on a day, that he went
out to his father to the reapers. And he said unto his
father, My head, my head. And he said to a lad, Carry
him to his mother. And when he had taken him, and
brought him to his mother, he sat on her knees till noon,
and then died. And she went up, and laid him on the bed
of the man of God, and shut the door upon him, and went
out.'[2] This case has usually been considered as one of
sunstroke or insolation, and this is probably the correct
view. But if the child's exclamation, ' My head, my

[1] 1 Kings xiii. 4-6.   [2] 2 Kings iv. 18-37.

head,' is to be understood as intimating sudden severe' pain of the head, it is possible that it may have been an instance of sudden *meningitis* (inflammation of the membranes of the brain) supervening in a delicate child. There are several varieties of sun-stroke, all of them endangering life, though many cases recover. In the severer form, or sun-stroke proper, the brain and nerve-centres are overwhelmed, the respiration and circulation are arrested, and death may ensue rapidly. The patient becomes unconscious, the pulse fails, and the skin is cold. Such cases, if not immediately fatal, often prove so in the course of a few hours. If eventually they recover, it is after a period of reaction accompanied by symptoms of severe injury to the nervous system. That death had actually occurred in this instance there can be no reasonable doubt. A period of ten or twelve hours at least must have elapsed before the arrival of the prophet. And it was not till after having kept the child on her knee till noon, and then seeing that he was dead, that the mother hastened to fetch Elisha. During her absence the child was laid on the bed of the prophet, and the door shut upon him; no remedies therefore were used, nor any attention given to the child. Gehazi, who arrived first at the house, on laying the prophet's staff on the face of the child, found there was 'neither voice nor hearing.' 'And when Elisha was come into the house, behold, the child was dead, and laid upon his bed.' The body was then cold, and it was not till after Elisha's prayer and stretching himself on the child, that 'the flesh of the child waxed warm,' and that subsequently he opened his eyes, after sneezing seven times. There are here no natural means, the use of which could explain the recovery.

CHAPTER VI.

MANY are the descriptions of old age that have been
given us by poets, philosophers, and physicians; but
none that excel in poetic beauty or graphic truthfulness that with which Solomon concludes the Book of
Ecclesiastes. Of this we give the Authorised Version,
introducing alterations of any importance adopted by the
Revised Version.

'Remember now (also) thy Creator in the days of thy
    youth,
While the evil days come not, nor the years draw nigh,
When thou shalt say, I have no pleasure in them ;
While the sun, or the light, or the moon, or the stars, be
    not darkened,
Nor the clouds return after the rain :
In the day when the keepers of the house shall tremble,
And the strong men shall bow themselves,
And the grinders cease because they are few,
And those that look out of the windows be darkened,
And the doors shall be shut in the streets, when the
    sound of the grinding is low,
And he (one) shall rise up at the voice of the bird,
And all the daughters of music shall be brought low;
And when (yea) they shall be afraid of that which is high,
And fears (terrors) shall be in the way,

And the almond tree shall flourish (blossom), and the
grasshopper shall be a burden,
And desire (the caper-berry) shall fail: because man
goeth to his long home,
And the mourners go about the streets:
Or ever the silver cord be loosed, or the golden bowl be
broken,
Or the pitcher be broken at the fountain, or the wheel
broken at the cistern.
Then shall the dust return to the earth as it was:
And the spirit shall return unto God who gave it.'

Whatever difficulty there may be in interpreting the
allegorical meaning of some of the poetic figures employed in this vivid picture of advanced age, one cannot
but be struck with the accurate delineation of the leading
features and the truthfulness of the whole. The law of
mortality is distinctly recognised, that man, like every
other organised being, has a period assigned to him for
his existence. He may escape the various dangers and
diseases by which that period is often cut short; but
sooner or later the very forces and materials by
which his life is sustained and by which his frame has
been developed, the slow but inevitable operation of
natural laws, end in the destruction of his material
organisation. His dust 'returns to the earth as it was.'
Not so, however, that which never was dust; the spirit,
as the Preacher knew, and does not fail to tell us,
'returns unto God who gave it,' spirit to Spirit!

The principle which we call life, with which all organised beings are endowed, and by which they are distinguished, enables them to impart the same principle
to materials derived from without, even, in the case of
plants, from the inorganic world, and incorporate them

with the original germ, and so build up and develop the future organism. The phenomena and changes attending this process occasion continual waste and change of material, and require corresponding supply. So long as the due relation between waste and supply is maintained, nutrition and the various functions of the body are maintained. But a time comes when waste exceeds supply, and when the various elements going to constitute the different fluids, tissues and organs no longer hold their due proportion; degradation and disorganisation ensue. The principle of life itself becomes enfeebled, and its power of imparting life to new material ceases. The animal and the plant alike cease to *live*—they *die*.

What is this principle, force or agent, which we call life, and which plays so grand and marvellous a part in the universe? To this question, science, as yet, has returned no response. Will it ever?

But mysterious as is the power, or agent, that imparts life to organic beings and transmits it from generation to generation, scarcely less mysterious is the gradual diminution and ultimate failure of this power to perpetuate the edifice which has been evolved from an almost imperceptible molecule, atom by atom, step by step, till it culminates in the full-grown man, that 'wondrous piece of work,' which, however,

> 'does not grow alone
> In thews and bulk; but, as this temple waxes,
> The inward service of the mind and soul
> Grows wide withal.'

Involution succeeds to evolution, and 'the paragon of animals, the beauty of the world,' proves to be but a 'body of humiliation,' a dissolving earthly tabernacle

for an inhabitant whose home 'is eternal in the heavens.'
As age advances man perceives that changes are taking
place in his bodily frame, rendering more and more difficult
the performance of his various functions and diminishing
his needed strength. It may be long ere any of the
more ordinary signs of disease are manifested, but at
last, even in the absence of such signs, 'Senectus ipsa
est morbus.'[1] Henceforth each day, each hour, is
marked by continuous incessant steps in the process
of destruction by which the individual lapses into the
universal.

The unity of our organisation is as remarkable as its
complexity. Not only is there a close interdependence
between the various organs and functions of our organic
life, but also a mutual relation between these and our
intelligence, and our life of relation to others and the
outer world. In the absence of any of the ordinary
causes of disease, it will depend on a variety of circumstances in what organ or function the first symptoms of
decay manifest themselves.

Not infrequently the first indications of impairment of
vitality are such as are connected with the mind and
nervous system, with which the Preacher begins his
description. The brain and nerves undergo important
changes in their physical constitution, the due supply of
healthy blood requisite for the maintenance of mental
and nervous functions begins to fail, the containing vessels
become rigid, congestion and rupture ensue, or the brain
wastes, softens, or becomes hard. But ere many of these
changes are manifested, weariness of mind and somnolency
betoken enfeebled mental power, and then 'The evil days
come and the years draw nigh,' when a man has no

---

[1] Terence, *Phormio*, Act iv. Sc. 1.

pleasure in them. The scenes and occupations of this life cease to charm. Even for 'Age that melts in unperceived decay,' if there are no pains, earthly pleasures are few and fleeting. Memory fails to recall even past joys, 'when the children were about us.' The nerves cease to vibrate in response to new impressions, and even care and anxieties no longer exercise their corroding influence.

The figurative terms in verse 2 have been differently interpreted. Impaired sight being referred to subsequently, it has been held that general mental obtuseness, impairment of the intellectual faculties and perceptive powers, are intended to be indicated by the darkening of the heavenly bodies. Even mental aberration, so frequent in very advanced age, it has been thought, is here signified. This appears to have been Mead's view, who says, 'Wisdom and understanding are frequently called light in the sacred Scriptures, and privation of reason darkness and blindness. Hence God is styled the Father of lights. Thus the virtues of the mind decaying may be compared to the luminaries of the world overcast.' Certainly this image of the darkening of the sun and moon and stars may be supposed to denote the gloom and sadness too often attending old age, whilst the return of the clouds after rain may very well typify the recurring troubles of the aged. If such views of verses 1 and 2 be accepted, they would be confined to the description of the mental characteristics of old age, those of the body being taken up in the following verses.

'The day when the keepers of the house shall tremble, and the strong men shall bow themselves,' indicates the time when the nutritive powers are no longer equal to the supply of material necessary to replace the waste that is constantly going on. Consequently the muscles shrivel and perish. The instruments of bodily strength and activity are unequal to anything beyond the moderate and regulated movements of common daily life. Muscular vigour required for defence no longer exists, and at length what is needed for sustaining the body erect fails. 'The strong men bow themselves,' and the gait becomes uncertain and tottering ; the keepers, or protectors, of the tenement tremble, in their feeble efforts to ward off danger. The solid framework of the house, the bones, become fragile, so as to break on any sudden or extra bodily effort. The character of the locomotion is altogether changed —'the child runs, the young man jumps, the adult marches, but the old man drags himself along.' The bolt shot from the bow bent by the young man's vigorous arm carries death to the enemy, but proves 'telum imbelle sine ictu,' when sent from the old man's hand.

'The grinders cease because they are few.' It is not necessary that we should confine the term grinders in this passage to the double or grinding teeth, though it is by these chiefly that the food is masticated and undergoes the first process in preparation for the other organs of digestion. There are several ways by which the number of the teeth is diminished in old age. They may decay and fall away piecemeal, or they may drop out from changes going on in the jaw and gums. As they are gradually lost, or become useless for their office, the sound of the grinding necessarily becomes low, when performed by the gums alone. The shutting of the street door, in association with the cessation of the sound of the mill, seems to indicate that the mouth is typified by the street door, for the opening and shutting of which there is less occasion when little food is taken, and when the sense of taste is blunted or lost. That failure of sight is meant by the darkening of 'those that look out of the windows,' we can have no doubt. Changes in the physical conformation of the eye, altering its character as an optical instrument, are among the very earliest indications of advancing life, requiring the artificial aid of glasses. But more serious effects ensue when the crystalline lens becomes opaque and gives rise to cataract. Then the house indeed becomes dark. Nor is this the only form of blindness met with in the aged. The function of the optic nerve itself may be lost, so that it no longer is influenced by light (*amaurosis*).

'All the daughters of music are brought low,' when the auditory nerve no longer responds to aerial vibrations. And this is the case when that chain of delicate and beautiful apparatus imbedded in the bony cavity of the internal ear is rendered immobile and unfitted for its office by ossification or other changes. But while entire loss of hearing is comparatively rare, merely as the result of senile change, impaired hearing is one of the commonest indications of advanced life, and with this is often asso-ciated a morbid irritation of the auditory nerve, giving rise to false sounds and leading the person to imagine that he hears noises, or persons speaking, startling or waking him up when no sounds have been heard. This singing in the ears (*tinnitus aurium*) may perhaps be what is implied by 'rising up at the voice of the bird,' though more probably this depicts the light and imperfect sleep of the aged. Old Barzillai says to David, 'Can I hear any more the voice of singing men and singing women?'

'They shall be afraid of that which is high, and terrors shall be in the way.' As fearlessness characterises the youth, and courage the strong man, so does timidity the aged. Mental vigour is often maintained when bodily strength is lost through age; but the brain, as the organ through which the mind acts, no longer being duly nourished, at length fails to answer the behests of the will. The mysterious union of the corporeal with the mental then is made manifest, that union which man cannot comprehend, but which nevertheless, as Augustine says, constitutes him man.[1]

The spirit may still be willing, but the flesh weak. There are no longer the insulated unbroken wires to transmit the electric current. We speak of imagination, invention, memory, and other intellectual faculties failing, when, for aught that we know, it is only the material instruments for their manifestation that have become unavailing. In certain forms of disease we know that this is the case. There are instances of cerebral disease attended by what is termed *aphasia* (loss of speech), not from any defect of power in the organs and muscles employed in articulation, nor from any mental incapacity to take in or respond to ideas. The intellect may be unimpaired, but the mandates of the will are interrupted in their passage to the organs that should and could give expression to them, had they received the mandates. Even in health and in every period of life we have evidence of the mysterious laws that regulate the interdependence of the physical and the psychical, though it is in extreme old age that we have the saddest illustrations.

'The almond tree shall blossom (or flourish), and the

---

[1] 'Modus quo corporibus adhærent spiritus, ... omnino mirus est, nec comprehendi ab homine potest; *et hoc ipse homo est.*' *De Civit. Dei*, xxi. 10.

grasshopper shall be a burden.' There is great difficulty
in interpreting the meaning of these words. Mead thinks
that as all the other senses have been mentioned, it is
not likely that the sense of smell would be omitted, and
endeavours to find here inability to derive pleasure from
agreeable odours of plants and flowers. The common
interpretation, which supposes that the almond blossom
represents the grey hairs of the aged, cannot, I think, be
supported. For, in the first place, the almond blossom
is not white, but pink, and grey hair is by no means
confined to old age, nor in the next place can either grey
hair or baldness be said to indicate blossoming or
flourishing or ripening of age. If the words would be
more correctly rendered,[1] 'the almond occasions loathing,'
i. e. 'this delicate fruit gives no pleasure to the old man,
whilst the locust, which every one else can eat, is a burden
or disgust to him,' the passage may be supposed to
refer both to the sense of smell and taste. The locust and
the grasshopper are both *Gryllidæ*, and the former, it is
well known, is eaten in the East both in the fresh and
dry state.

'And desire (the caper-berry) shall fail, because man
goeth to his long home.' If the word which the A.V.
translates 'desire' is correctly rendered by the LXX
κάππαρις, and by the R. V. caper-berry, we can only
assume that this berry, so frequently used as a condiment
and stimulant, is to be taken as the representative of the
various agents had recourse to in order to rouse the
failing appetite, or desire, for all forms of sensual enjoy-
ment, because man is going to his long home.[2]

---

[1] *Annotated Par. Bible* (R. T. S.) *in loco*.
[2] Capers were held by the Arabians to be aphrodisiacal, and are, I believe,
so considered by the Jews in the present day. Vide Paulus Ægineta, Adams,
Syd. Soc. Trans., vol. iii. p. 156, and references to Rhases and Avicenna.

The loosening of the silver cord may with tolerable certainty be taken as descriptive of the impaired function of the spinal cord and its accessories, which is the essential cause of many of the infirmities of the aged.

The remaining figures Mead characterises as true enigmas requiring an Œdipus to solve them, and his own attempts are certainly not successful. It is true that the circulation of the blood was unknown in Solomon's time, but the heart was known to be a receptacle or fountain of blood, and that in some way or other it was connected with machinery for distribution of its contents. The broken pitcher and wheel are, at all events, fit emblems, in the present day, to describe the heart's failure and the feeble and deranged circulatory powers which are so often the immediate precursors of the final stopping of the wheel of life. The cranium, as containing so important an organ as the brain, may fitly be termed 'the golden bowl,' and the more important paralytic affections of the aged we know are associated with disease of the cerebral vessels and disorganisation of the brain substance.

The Psalmist tells us that 'the days of our years are threescore years and ten, and if by reason of strength they be fourscore years, yet is their strength labour and sorrow.'[1]

It is a question that has been discussed, whether in the present day of advanced science and civilization and improved hygienic rules, the normal duration of human life has, or has not, been prolonged beyond the limits laid down by the Psalmist. But there can be

In Syria this berry is of a much more acrid and stimulant character than as cultivated in this country.

[1] Psalm xc. 10.

no question that it is incumbent on the aged to recognise
the necessity for observing those laws and precepts
which are established by both science and experience.
'Peu de gens savent être vieux' was a ṣaying of La
Rochefoucauld.   No doubt the lesson is one often
difficult to learn, and both science and religion impress
on us the need we have to pray, 'So teach us to
number our days, that we may apply our hearts unto
wisdom.'   This wisdom in regard to the past and the
present, as well as to the future, it behoves the aged to
acquire.   For them the injunction 'Know thyself' implies,
'I have been young, and now am old,' and not less
certainly that even the present hour is not for them
what once it was.   ' Jam non tua.'

CHAPTER VII.

PHYSICAL CAUSE OF THE DEATH OF CHRIST.

THE death of Christ on the cross being the central fact of the Christian religion, with which all other facts and all its doctrines are in essential vital relation, it will be admitted that every fact and every consideration that tends to confirm and elucidate that momentous event must be of supreme interest and importance. It is, therefore, not a little surprising that, until the appearance of Dr. Stroud's work,[1] the result of prolonged labour and learned research, no adequate attempt should have been made to demonstrate the nature of the immediate, essential, physical cause of the death of the Saviour. No doubt the more accurate and advanced physiological science of recent times has given superior advantages for the investigation of a subject which was long held to be surrounded by difficulties and obscurity. That the conclusions to which Dr. Stroud has arrived are valid and incontrovertible will, we think, be admitted by all who are competent to judge both of the facts that he adduces and the soundness of the inductive reasoning by which he arrives at his conclusions.

As, however, there is reason to think that the light which has now been shed on this sacred subject is not so generally known as is desirable, we have deemed it not

[1] *Treatise on the Physical Cause of the Death of Christ and its relations to the Principles and Practice of Christianity*, by W. Stroud, M.D., London, 1847.

inappropriate to present our readers, as a supplement to the subjects of which we have already treated, with a short account of the physical cause of our Lord's death, as demonstrated mainly through the researches of Dr. Stroud.

That the question is not one of mere curious interest, but has important bearings both on Christian evidences and doctrine, will be manifest on the slightest reflection. We, however, restrict ourselves, as far as may be, to what, without irreverence, may be called the scientific or medical aspect of the subject, and desire *in limine* to acknowledge, with Dr. Stroud, in the fullest manner, the union of the Divine and human nature in Christ, and that it is only with what relates to His perfect human nature, which alone could be subject to suffering and death, that we have here to do. The accounts given us by the four Evangelists, although not the only, are the chief, sources of information afforded to us by the Scriptures, and the combined evidence derived from both the Old and the New Testament shows that the whole transaction was extraordinary and unique.

' Many centuries before the event, the voice of pro- phecy had proclaimed that the Saviour of mankind would suffer a death at once violent and voluntary, as a criminal, and as a victim, universally approved by God and man, yet loaded with the malediction of both. His death was to be directed by Jewish priests without power, and executed by Gentile rulers without authority, and He was to be condemned on a charge in which, notwith- standing their religious hostility, both parties could unite in attesting and rejecting His claims as the Messiah. He was to suffer the death of the cross, which commonly happened by slow exhaustion, and in Judea was usually hastened by breaking the legs, yet none of His bones were to be broken. His heart was at the same time to be pierced, and He was to die suddenly, as a sin-offering by the effusion of His life's blood, the appointed means of atonement, although the former was not essential to the punishment of crucifixion, and the latter was the very reverse of its usual effect. The actual accomplishment of all these intricate and apparently discordant conditions is formally asserted in various parts of the New Testament not as a casual coincidence, but as indispensably necessary to the fulfilment of prophecy, the veracity of which would have been forfeited had any one of them failed to take place.'[1]

The principal causes to which the death of Christ was attributed by the older commentators and others were (1) the ordinary sufferings attendant on crucifixion ; (2) an unusual degree of bodily weakness ; (3) the wound inflicted by the soldier's spear; (4) supernatural interposition.

1. That the death of Christ should very generally have been supposed, by those who derived their knowledge of crucifixion as a punishment from the evangelical records alone, to have resulted from the ordinary and necessary sufferings attending that mode of execution is not surprising. But to obtain correct notions on this subject we must have recourse to other historical sources of information. These, indeed, clearly show that crucifixion was a peculiarly painful, lingering, and ignominious form of punishment, but that the sufferings, though great, have, either through ignorance or design, been much exaggerated. Numerous instances may be adduced from both ancient and modern authors in proof of its

<hr>

[1] Stroud, p. 29.

lingering nature, especially from the Roman Martyrology. From Origen and others of the early Fathers it would appear that two days was the usual period during which crucified persons survived, when death was not hastened by additional means. This is the period during which St. Andrew the apostle is reported to have lived on the cross, and which time he is said to have spent in preaching to the people. Victor, Bishop of Amiternum, who was crucified with his head downwards, a position which must have been unfavourable to life, survived the same period.[1]

In other recorded instances the sufferers have survived three days, and some even longer, though subjected to additional torture. From the examination of numerous recorded cases it appears that, in the absence of any extra cruelty beyond simple crucifixion, death seldom occurred within two days.

Jesus, however, died suddenly after enduring the suffering of the cross only six hours, whilst the malefactors crucified along with Him lived till their legs were broken. Pilate therefore, knowing this, 'marvelled if He were already dead,' and enquired of the centurion 'whether He had been any while dead,' when Joseph of Arimathea came and craved the body of Jesus. The application which the Jews made to Pilate, 'that their legs might be broken,' lest the bodies should remain on the cross during the Sabbath, was evidently prompted by the belief that otherwise death would not have ensued soon enough to avoid the infringement of their law.

2. 'His last sufferings befell Him when in the flower of His age, at the period of His greatest vigour and maturity.

---

[1] Jacobus Bosius, *Crux Triumphans et Gloriosa*, pp. 8, 9, 43 et seq. See also numerous detailed references given by Dr. Stroud from both ancient and modern writers, and, among others, from Ellis in his *History of Madagascar*.

Those in the garden of Gethsemane, although intense, were of short duration, and He was supernaturally strengthened for the very purpose of enabling Him to support them. Those incidental to crucifixion were not more severe in His case than in that of others. His deportment throughout the whole scene, whether in the garden, before the tribunal of the Sanhedrim and of Pilate, or at Golgotha, evinced the utmost piety, fortitude and self-possession. The circumstance of Simon the Cyrenian being compelled to assist in bearing His cross by no means proves that mere weakness disabled Christ from bearing it alone. The contrary appears, from His immediately afterwards addressing the Jewish women who bewailed His fate, and bidding them weep not for Him, but for themselves and their children. On arriving at the fatal spot He refused the cup of medicated wine usually given as a cordial to crucified persons; and after praying for His executioners, assuring the penitent malefactor of eternal happiness, providing for the future support of His widowed mother, and actively concurring in the fulfilment of prophecy, He suddenly expired amidst loud and fervent ejaculations, which alone were sufficient to show that He retained all His faculties of mind and body to the last moment of His life.'[1]

3. The contention of Granville Penn and others, that the death of Christ resulted from the wound inflicted by the soldier's spear, is mainly supported by a various reading of the Vatican and some other MSS., which interpose between verses 49 and 50 of Matthew's account the words, 'But another taking a spear, pierced His side, and there came forth water and blood.' This reading, however, is not generally accepted, and is not adopted

---

[1] Stroud, p. 71.

either by the A. V. or the R. V.,[1] though given by the latter in a note. But 'though excluded by almost all the ancient MS. versions and Fathers, and rejected by the principal critics and editors of the Greek Testament,' it was adopted by Chrysostom. In the opinion of Dr. Stroud and others, 'it is an unwarrantable interpolation in Matthew's Gospel of words borrowed from that of John, and stamped with internal marks of inconsistency and falsehood.' But even Chrysostom, maintaining as he did that Christ laid down His life by His own power, represents the spear-wound as having been inflicted on the body after death, of which proof will be adduced when we come to speak of the true physical cause of the death.

How inconsistent are the words as interpolated in Matthew's account both with what precedes and what follows, a careful reader will see, and has been fully shown by Dr. Stroud, whereas their position in the narrative of John, who specially emphasises the fact that he was an eye-witness of the events, is perfectly consistent with his record. An additional reason against the spear-wound having been inflicted during life is afforded by the fact that the soldiers were not at liberty to interfere with the execution at their pleasure. It was only when they believed that Christ was already dead, and that there was no necessity for them to carry out the command to break the legs, that the spear was employed to make certain the fact of death having already taken place.

4. That none of the views to which we have alluded have been considered tenable is shown by the prevalence, from the earliest times to the present day, of the opinion that it is to supernatural agency that the death of Christ is to be attributed. Tertullian, Origen, and many others

[1] Nor by Segond in the New French Version.

of the ancient Christian writers, and of the most eminent among modern commentators, have maintained that Christ by a voluntary supernatural power 'laid down His life,' 'dismissed His spirit,' 'resigned His spirit,' 'let go His soul and delivered it up into the hands of God,' 'that His life was not forcibly extorted from Him but freely resigned.' These and similar expressions have been employed by those who believe that it was not by the intervention of any physical cause that the human life of Christ was extinguished. That it was not through force of necessity, but that He died freely and voluntarily when His nature was in full strength, must, it is thought, have been the conviction of the centurion when he exclaimed, 'Truly this was the Son of God.' We need not say how many passages of Scripture may be cited which seem to support such views. Our Lord Himself says, 'No man taketh My life from Me, but I lay it down of Myself.'

That this long-prevalent view, which assigns the Lord's death to supernatural agency, is inconsistent with His own language when speaking to His disciples, and with the teaching of Scripture in many places both of the Old and New Testament, is manifest. But it is not within our scope to enter on the discussion of the theological questions which are involved in any attempt to harmonise the various all-important Scriptural statements relating to the death of Him who offered Himself a sacrifice for the sins of the world, and who by 'wicked hands was crucified and slain.'

If none of the causes to which we have referred can be deemed to afford an adequate explanation of the immediate cause of our Lord's death, we naturally ask what other cause was there that can be both held to be sufficient and consistent with the circumstances of the case? To this Dr. Stroud has replied, *Agony of mind, producing rupture of the heart.* The outline of the argument by which he has been led to this conclusion we give in his own words:

'In the garden of Gethsemane Christ endured mental agony so intense that, had it not been limited by Divine interposition, it would probably have destroyed. His life without the aid of any other sufferings; but having been thus mitigated, its effects were confined to violent palpitation of the heart, accompanied with bloody sweat. On the cross this agony was renewed, in conjunction with the ordinary sufferings incidental to that mode of punishment; and having at this time been allowed to proceed to its utmost extremity without restraint, occasioned sudden death by rupture of the heart, intimated by a discharge of blood and water from His side, when it was afterwards pierced with a spear.'[1]

The heart, which is the central and main power by which the circulation of the blood is effected, is a muscular organ consisting of four distinct chambers, through which the blood enters from all regions of the system and passes out to be distributed by the arteries throughout the body to the most remote parts. But though it is made up of muscular fibres it is not, like other muscles, under the control of the will. It is what is termed an 'involuntary muscle'; its requisite, ordained, regular action going on incessantly, so long as life lasts, uncontrolled by the will. Fixed only at its base, on which the rest of the organ moves, the free, uncontrolled action of its different compartments is secured by its being enclosed in an envelope, or sac, termed the 'pericardium,' the interior of which is lubricated by a thin

[1] Stroud.

clear secretion to obviate friction. But whilst its constant rhythmical action is maintained independent of the will, it manifests, more than any other organ of our body, that intimate connexion which exists between body and mind. Of this every one is more or less conscious. Hence the various current phrases employed to denote the effects of the passions and varying mental states on the heart's action, such as ' My heart jumps for joy,' ' My heart feels light ; ' ' it is oppressed, it is heavy, it is ready to break ; ' all indicating conscious disturbance of the heart induced by mental causes. Every physician knows that such phrases are not merely metaphorical, but that they really express actual derangements of the heart's action and condition, and often such as indicate danger to life. A fit of passion, sudden grief or joy, fear or terror, intense mental anxiety or strain, especially that which attends conflicting emotions, may through the medium of the heart so derange all the vital functions as to imperil and destroy life. The symptoms attending such disturbance vary with the character of the mental exciting causes, sometimes indicating dangerous over-excitement and action, and at others even more dangerous depression and failure of action. As the result of exciting passions we have forcible beating of the heart and rapid pulse, glowing features, glistening eye, quick breathing, giddiness, and headache. Depressing passions are attended by a feeble, scarcely discernible pulse, faint, tremulous action of the heart, pale features, profuse sweating, and gasping breath, ending in a swoon and final stoppage of the heart's action.

In all these dangerous forms of cardiac derangement there may be no actual structural disease of the heart, though every physician knows how difficult it often is to persuade a patient of this, who happens to be the frequent subject of palpitation and irregular action and sense of pain or discomfort about the heart, from various and especially moral causes. If, however, there be actual disease of the organ, any source of disturbed action becomes doubly dangerous, and many cases of sudden death occur from comparatively trivial exciting causes where the actual cardiac disease is of a very limited and apparently slight character. But the danger of actual rupture of the organ is greatest where, from impaired nutrition, its muscular power is seriously weakened; and of all causes inducing such disease none are more powerful than prolonged distressing and depressing mental states. The patient may often then be truly said to ' die of a broken heart.'

Assuming that the heart is in all respects sound and vigorous, the danger attending prolonged intense mental agony is yet great, for not only may rupture of the heart even then be the result, though effected in a somewhat different way, but the tension exerted on the whole circulating system may be such as to rupture the smaller vessels of the lungs or brain, or those supplying the surface of the body, and thus occasion hæmorrhage. There can be no doubt that death has often occurred in one or other of these ways, though it may be admitted that in the majority of cases there has been evidence of pre-existing cardiac disease.

A careful study of what is recorded as having transpired in the garden of Gethsemane is of the utmost importance in connexion with our subject, and it should be remembered that this account is given by Luke the physician. In his Gospel, chap. xxii. verses 41–44, we read (R.V.): 'And He was parted from them about a

stone's cast ; and He kneeled down and prayed, saying,
Father, if Thou be willing, remove this cup from Me :
nevertheless not My will, but Thine, be done. And there
appeared unto Him an angel from heaven, strengthening
Him. And being in an agony He prayed more earnestly :
and His sweat became as it were great drops of blood
falling down upon the ground.'[1] In these verses there are
terms employed which are strictly medical, and not used
elsewhere in the New Testament. The radical meaning
of the Greek word rendered 'agony' is struggling or
contention, and is described by Galen, the Greek medical
authority,[2] as a mental conflict between anger and fear,
the one tending to drive the blood outwards and the
other inwards to the vital organs, with corresponding
outward pallor and coldness. Speaking generally, it
implies a conflict between divers and contrary mental
states, e. g. an impulse to resist danger and fear to
encounter it. Thus in our Lord's case it would be the
fitting expression to denote the severe mental struggle
'between the terror of death and the judicial anger of
the righteous Father.' 'Father, if Thou be willing,
remove this cup from Me ; nevertheless not My will,
but Thine, be done.'

The Greek word which both the A.V. and the R.V.
render 'great drops' is θρόμβοι, which, in a general sense,
means a concrete mass or lump of the solid constituents
of a liquid, such as milk or blood. In the technical
sense, in which it is used by Hippocrates and other
medical authorities, it means a drop or mass of coagu-
lated blood. In medical phraseology of the present day,

---

[1] Καὶ γενόμενος ἐν ἀγωνίᾳ ἐκτενέστερον προσηύχετο· ἐγένετο δὲ ὁ ἱδρὼς
αὐτοῦ ὡσεὶ θρόμβοι αἵματος καταβαίνοντες ἐπὶ τὴν γῆν, v. 44.

[2] *De Symptom Caus.* ii. 5, tom. vii. p. 192.

I

a 'thrombus' is a clot of blood blocking up the calibre of a blood-vessel.

The adverb ὡσεὶ, translated 'as it were,' would seem to imply that the drops which fell to the ground were not pure blood, but merely sweat (ἰδρὼς) mixed with the colouring particles of the blood, and thus only resembling blood, though some authorities say that the adverbs ὡς and ὡσεὶ do sometimes imply reality.

Sudden and abnormally profuse sweating, as the result of intense mental excitement and anxiety, is of sufficiently common occurrence to be well known, and there are numerous cases on record in which such sweating has been bloody. In the *Ephemerides* several examples are given of bloody tears, as well as sweat, occasioned by extreme dread of death. Tissot reports the case of a sailor who was so alarmed in a storm that, through fear of death, he fell down and his face sweated blood, which, during the whole continuance of the storm, returned like ordinary sweat as fast as it was wiped away.[1] In a case cited by Schenck from a martyrology, a nun, who was threatened by armed soldiers with instant death, was so terrified and agitated that she discharged blood from every part of her body, and died of hæmorrhage in the sight of her assailants.[2] It would be easy from modern medical records to adduce evidence of hæmorrhage similarly induced, from small vessels supplying internal organs, such as the brain, occasioning rapid death.

Now the record tells us that the Divine Sufferer, 'when exceeding sorrowful even unto death,' 'sore amazed and very heavy,' 'being in an agony, He prayed more earnestly,' and was rescued by supernatural inter-

---

[1] Tissot's *Traité des Nerfs, &c.*, pp. 279, 280.
[2] *J. Schenck à Grafenberg Observ. Med. &c.*, lib. iii. p. 458.

position from the danger by which He was then threatened — 'an angel from heaven strengthening Him.'[1]

The sufferings in Gethsemane, overwhelming as they were, and threatening immediate death, were, however, wholly mental—anguish of soul. As yet the Saviour had been subjected to no bodily suffering from the hand of man. It was otherwise in the succeeding hours, previous to and during crucifixion. Bodily suffering of no ordinary kind was then superadded, though, for reasons already adduced, not such as afford us a satisfactory explanation of the death as it is recorded to have taken place. Doubtless the mental agony lasted, even if in a mitigated degree, throughout the proceedings that ended in His being condemned to die ; but when on the cross it reached its utmost intensity, and drew forth the bitter exclamation, ' My God ! my God ! why hast Thou forsaken Me ?' The cup then again presented was drunk to the very dregs. No supernatural relief then interposing, the violence of the strain on the heart was such as to occasion the rupture of its walls, with sudden suppression of all circulation, and so preventing such hæmorrhagic signs as occurred in the garden. The immediate consequence of rupture of the heart would be the effusion of blood into the pericardium. The amount poured out would depend on the extent and character of the ruptured opening. In similar cases the amount effused has been at once so great as, by its pressure around the whole organ, combined with the shock, to produce instant death. In other instances the quantity first effused has been small,

---

[1] The terms used by the Evangelists in their descriptions, especially by Mark, are, in the opinion of competent judges, the strongest which the Greek language could supply.

but repeated at each beat, the heart continuing to act for an hour or more before life has been extinct. The suddenness of Christ's death leads to the belief that the rent was large, and the violence of the heart's contraction being great, as the result of its previous strong and healthy condition, the amount of blood effused would be large. The perfect consciousness of the Sufferer, as indicated by His knowledge of what yet remained of prophecy to be fulfilled, and the loud voice with which He cried when uttering His last words, immediately preceding the bowing of His head and resigning His spirit, contra-indicate gradual exhaustion of mind or body, whether from hæmorrhage or any other cause.

In order to understand what immediately followed on the wound by the soldier's spear, it is necessary to explain what is meant by coagulation of the blood, although the laws by which this is governed, being connected with the principle of life, are still obscure. In the living and healthy state the blood is a uniform fluid consisting largely of water, containing albumen and fibrin, along with certain saline constituents and numerous organised particles termed 'red globules,' which give to it its colour and play an important part in the vital functions that it fulfils. The appearance of this uniform red fluid while flowing, or as first shed, is known to all; and this appearance it presents so long as it is contained within the heart and blood-vessels during life. But on the failure of these conditions it undergoes a remarkable change. When discharged from its containing cavities and vessels, it soon loses its vitality and separates into distinct portions. The fibrin spontaneously concretes into a spongy mass, in which the red globules are entangled, and which floats or sinks in the fluid portion termed serum, containing the water and the albumen with the other constituents. Thus in a short time blood drawn from the arm into a basin presents the appearance of blood and water, but the technical terms for which would be *crassamentum* and *serum*. The time required for this coagulation and separation of the constituents of the blood is very short, after it has passed out of the heart or any of the containing vessels. We cannot say precisely what length of time elapsed between the utterance of the Saviour's last words and the piercing of His side by the spear; but whilst it could not have been more than two hours, calculating the time before sunset, it was not sufficient for the coagulation of blood that might still have been retained in the heart or large vessels, but was amply sufficient had it been poured into the pericardium through rupture of the walls of the heart; for we know that in such circumstances the time required for coagulation would not differ materially from that required when out of the body.

We conclude, therefore, with the writer whose line of argument we have followed,[1] 'that it may with certainty be affirmed that between the agony of mind which the Saviour endured in the garden of Gethsemane, and the profuse sweat mixed with clotted blood which so rapidly followed it, violent palpitation of the heart must necessarily have intervened; this being the only known condition which could have been at once the effect of the former occurrence, and the cause of the latter. In like manner, when on the cross this agony was renewed, and by the addition of bodily suffering was increased to the utmost intensity, no other known condition could have formed the connecting link between that mental anguish and

[1] Stroud, pp. 155, 156.

His sudden death, preceded by loud exclamations, and followed by an effusion of blood and water from His side when afterwards pierced with a spear, than the aggravation even to rupture, of the same violent action of the heart, of which the previous palpitation and bloody sweat were but a lower degree and a natural prelude. If, whilst every other explanation hitherto offered has been shown to be untenable, the cause now assigned for the death of Christ, namely, *rupture of the heart from agony of mind*, has been proved to be the result of an actual power in nature, fully adequate to the effect, really present without counteraction, minutely agreeing with all the facts of the case, and necessarily implied by them, this cause must, according to the principles of inductive reasoning, be regarded as demonstrated.'

We must refer to the latter portions of Dr. Stroud's able treatise those who are anxious to satisfy themselves how far the view here set forth harmonises with the statements of Scripture on the doctrine of the Atonement, with the types and prophecies relating to the death of Christ, with the narratives and symbols of the New Testament, and generally with Scriptural doctrine, in relation to this central fact of Christianity.

APPENDIX.

FIERY SERPENTS.

THE punishment inflicted on the children of Israel by means of the fiery serpents with which they were visited, in consequence of their murmuring against the Lord and Moses, scarcely comes within the scope of our subject. But the curious and novel explanation which Küchenmeister[1] has attempted to give of the brief Biblical account seems deserving of notice, as it is but little known. In Numbers xxi. 4 we read, 'And they journeyed from Mount Hor by the way of the Red Sea, to compass the land of Edom ; and the soul of the people was much discouraged because of the way. And the people spake against God and against Moses.' 'And the Lord sent fiery serpents among the people, and they bit the people, and much people of Israel died.' In Deut. viii. 15 the same visitation is recorded—'Who led thee through that great and terrible wilderness, wherein were fiery serpents, and scorpions, and drought, where there was no water.' In the prophecies of Isaiah only do we hear of '*flying* fiery serpents' along with the 'viper.'[2]

The Hebrew generic term for the serpent tribe is נָחָשׁ, translated by the LXX ὄφις. There has been

---

[1] *Manual of Parasites.* Syden. Soc. Edition. Vol. i. p. 390.
[2] Isaiah xxx. 6 and xiv. 29.

much discussion as to the particular species by whose bite much people died, without, however, any trustworthy decision having been arrived at. Some have considered it to be the διψάς, one of the *Colubers*, whose bite is attended by burning pain and inflammatory eruption and great thirst. There is no true flying serpent, although some have the faculty of darting from a distance at the object of their attack. But there is a species of Haye or hooded serpent, which has the power of distending the hood in the form of wings at the side of the head. This or an allied species of serpent is met with at the Cape, and called the 'Pof or Spooch Adder.' In some of the symbolical pictures of the Egyptians there are serpents represented with wings like a bird. The specific term 'fiery' might very well be applied to several serpents met with in the desert of Arabia, whose bite is followed by burning pain, and one of these is supposed to be the שָׂרָף of Numbers xxi, the ὄφεις τοὺς θανατοῦντας or deadly serpents of the LXX, which can dart from branch to branch of a tree, or fling themselves to the ground.

Now Küchenmeister contends that the Hebrew words rendered 'fiery serpents' ought to have the article before each word οἱ ὄφεις οἱ σεράφιμ, and that as seraphim is derived from שָׂרָף, it merely signifies that which burns ('is qui comburit'). He therefore thinks it is clear that a 'species of animal is referred to, which is distinguished by the inflammability of its bite, or generally by the inflammation which its presence occasions.' He further maintains that the mode in which הַנְּחָשִׁים הַשְּׂרָפִים annoyed the people is described in the seventh verse: 'Therefore the people came to Moses, and said, We have sinned, for we have spoken against the Lord, and against thee. Pray unto the Lord, that He take away the serpents from us.' The last clause, he says, should be rendered 'that Jehovah may allow to be taken away from upon us.' This he believes is not descriptive of the attacks of snakes, which when they inflict wounds do it without remaining upon the person; they come to him unseen, but not upon him. But it suits very well the *Filaria Medinensis*, as its seat is immediately beneath the skin, where it gives rise to boils and tumours upon the surface.

This parasitic worm, the *Filaria Medinensis*, or guinea-worm, was in ancient times reckoned among the serpents, on account of its snake-like form, and was named by the Greeks δρακόντιον = *dracunculus*, i. e. a species of snake which had something fabulous and inexplicable about it, and which, though from its form it might be considered a serpent, could not with equal propriety, from its nature, pass as a snake. The inflammatory pain and swelling which occur with the breaking out of the worm are very well expressed by ' seraphim.'

The *dracunculus*, or guinea-worm, has long been known as endemic on the borders of the Red Sea and in the Arabian desert. The first notice of it appears to have been given by Agatharchides[1], who is quoted by Plutarch[2] as narrating that 'the people taken ill near the Red Sea suffered from many strange and unheard-of attacks; amongst others little snakes came out upon them (δρακόντια μικρὰ), which gnawed away their legs and arms, and when touched again retracted themselves up

---

[1] A Greek writer on geography who lived in the second century B.C., the fragments of whose works contain a great deal of information regarding the Nile and the Red Sea.

[2] *Sympos.* viii. 9.

in the muscles, and there gave rise to the most insupport-
able inflammations.'

This is a correct description of the attacks of a now
well-known parasite which is endemic in many parts of
the East, and sometimes assumes an epidemic character,
as we may suppose was the case during the time of the
Exodus, if we can entertain the view of Küchenmeister
and some others.

The following are the characters of this parasite,
commonly called *dracunculus*, or guinea-worm, but now
classed with the *Filariæ*, or threadlike worms (*filum*, a
thread). It usually measures from one to three feet in
length, but examples have been met with measuring six
feet. In breadth it is about one-tenth of an inch. In
the adult state it is believed to obtain entrance into the
body of a person through those parts which are most
exposed, especially the feet and legs. When introduced
into the system by drinking infected water, the worm
developes in the intestinal canal, and subsequently makes
its way to the surface, and this probably is the chief
mode by which it obtains entrance. The presence of
the worms is first denoted by the pain and inflammation
attending their attempted exit through the skin, which
becomes swollen and inflamed around the point at which
they appear, especially if by unskilful attempts to extract
them the worm is broken and a portion left behind. To
avoid this, the old method employed by the Persians is
still in use. By gentle and continuous traction the
exposed portion of the worm is wound around a small
stick or bone, till at successive intervals the whole is
wound on to the stick and so extracted.

In certain districts the ponds and stagnant pools swarm
with microscopic organisms, among which the guinea-

worm often abounds. There is then certainly no im-
probability in the supposition that the Israelites, when
suffering from drought, as we know they did, would be
likely, from seizing on any water, however foul, to become
infested with the *Filaria*, which from its general form
might be spoken of as a serpent, and denominated fiery
from its inflammatory and painful effects. And it is
certainly more easy to understand how, in this way,
large numbers of people should be destroyed rather than
by serpent bites in the ordinary way in which they are
inflicted. Serpents exist in comparatively small numbers
in any locality, and are generally easily seen and guarded
against, and whilst their mortal effects are rapidly induced, they are not generally attended by much pain
and inflammation, but rather by stupor and depression.

'The *Filaria Medinensis*,' says a recent writer,[1] 'is
met with throughout the western half of the Arabian
peninsula, from the most northern part of the Hedjaz
province to Aden, and both in the burning sandy plains
and mountainous districts. Of 3500 to 4000 Turkish
soldiers of an expeditionary force visiting for four months
the country of Djebel Chahare in 1877, no less than 2500
men were attacked, and there was an average of four
worms in each man, whilst some had 10, 20, 30, or more.
The exhausted soldiers on the march got them from
drinking of the stagnant pools. The length of the worms
was from 4 to 48 inches.'

How far Küchenmeister's view is admissible or satisfactory, we leave to the reader to determine. But
whatever opinion may be held as to the particular
creature through whose agency the people died, it
cannot affect the more important part of the record,

<hr/>

[1] Sambolsky, *Du Ver de Medine*, 1879.

which relates to the means by which the mortality was stayed.

'And the Lord said unto Moses, Make thee a fiery serpent and set it upon a pole ; and it shall come to pass that every one that is bitten, when he looketh upon it, shall live. And Moses made a serpent of brass, and put it upon a pole, and it came to pass that if a serpent had bitten any man, when he beheld the serpent of brass he lived.'

Whatever similitude of form there may be between the *Filaria* and a serpent, we can scarcely doubt that the brazen image erected by Moses was that of a serpent. Various important considerations would lead us to conclude that the symbol employed was that of a serpent. But it is sufficient to recall the precious use which our Lord makes of the miracle recorded by His servant, in His ever to be remembered words to Nicodemus :

'And as Moses lifted up the serpent (τὸν ὄφιν) in the wilderness, even so must the Son of man be lifted up : That whosoever believeth in Him should not perish, but have eternal life. For God so loved the world that He gave His only begotten Son, that whosoever believeth in Him should not perish, but have everlasting life.'

NOTES.

Introduction.—Of the medical science and practice of the Jews in the time of our Lord, Dr. Stapfer says : ' Tout le monde s'occupait de médecine et personne n'en savait le premier mot. La médecine existait en Grèce depuir cinq cent ans, mais elle n'en était pas sortie. L'ignorancs des Juifs en médecine et leur impuissance à s'affranchie de cette ignorance venaient de ce qu'ils voyaient dans la maladie la punition de péchés commis soit par le patient lui-même, soit par ses parents et qu'ils l'attribuaient presque toujours à l'influence d'un mauvais esprit. La seule guérison possible était alors l'expulsion du démon (ou des démons, quelquefois on en avait plusieurs), et toute la science médicale se réduisait à chercher le meilleur mode d'expulsion. Ce n'était pas le plus instruit qui était le plus propre à cette œuvre de bienfaisance, mais le plus religieux.'—*La Palestine au temps de Jésus Christ*, par Edm. Stapfer ; Paris, 1885, 3rd edition, p. 243.

Leprosy.—I am indebted to my friend Dr. Greenhill for the following references in ancient writings to the subject of Leprosy.

'*Lepra* cutis asperitas squammosa lepidi similis (unde et nomen sumpsit), cujus color nunc in ingredinem vertitur, nunc in alborem, nunc in ruborem.'—Isidorus Hispal. *Etymol.* lib. iv. cap. 8. § 11. tom. i. p. 98, ed. Matr. 1778.

'Scabies, et lepra, utraque passio, asperitas cutis cum pruritu et squammatione.'—Ibid. § 10.

'Elephantiacus morbus dicitur ex similitudine elephantis,' etc.—Ibid. § 12.

Lepra symbolical of sin.—Gregor. Nazian. *Orat.* xl. tom. i. p. 662, C., ed. Colon. 1690.

Leprosy in man, and also in house, symbolical of sin.— Tertull. *On Modesty* (vol. iii. p. 115 ; Clark's ed. ; Edinb. 1870), cap. 20. tom. i. p. 840, ed. Oehler, Lips. 1853.

Leprosy in man, and in house, symbolical of sin, and 'of Jews' synagogue.'—Origen, *Selecta in Levit.* tom. ix. p. 167, &c.; ed. Lommatzseh, Berol. 1839.

Leprosy symbolical of sin; and when all over the body and clean signifies τῆς ἀληθείας ἁπλοῦν χρῶμα.—Clem. Alex. *Pædag.* lib. iii. cap. 11. p. 286, ed. Venet. 1757. (Vid. Phil. *Lib. de Plantat.* § 26. tom. i. p. 346, ed. Mangey.)

'Lepra doctrina est falsa.' Leprosi are heretics and six kinds of leprosy correspond to different heresies.— Isidorus Hispal. *Myst. Exposit. Sacram.,* seu 'Quæst. in *Levit.*' cap. 11, tom. ii. p. 237.

'Nemo variet, nemo leprosus sit. Doctrina inconstans, non habens unum colorem, mentis lepram significat: et istam Christus mundat.'—St. August. *Sermo* clxxvii. tom. v. p. 1217. D., ed. Paris, 1837.

Leprosy in the house.—'Men, clothes, and stones have not the same sort of diseases; but the names of human diseases are by analogy (or, as the Grammarian terms it, by figure of speech) applied to the diseases of other things. In Berne, for instance, they speak of the *cancer of buildings*, but then that is not the distemper so called in the human body. The *cancer of buildings* is with equal propriety a Swiss, as the *leprosy of buildings* is a Hebrew, expression . . . . [In Egypt] two sorts of diseases of certain trees, proceeding from insects, are there termed *leprosy* . . . . Hasselquist likewise has (in p. 221 of his *Travels in the Holy Land*) spoken of a *leprosy* in the fig-trees.'—Michaelis, *Commentaries on the Laws of Moses,* vol. iii. p. 288 ; Lond. 1814.

Diseases of the Nervous System, p. 81.—The R. V. translates σεληνιάζεται in Matt. xvii. 15 'epileptic,' and not lunatic, as given in the A. V. But if this new reading be accepted as the more correct, the subject of the miracle was none the less 'insane,' even if the words 'and the devil (or demon) went out from him' imply something more than ordinary insanity. The new French Version of Dr. L. Segond retains the term 'lunatique,' and says, 'Jésus menaça le démon qui sortit de lui.'

Wool-sorters' Disease, p. 53.—Although the disease
thus called has only recently become known to us, my
friend Dr. Aquila Smith has favoured me with some
extracts from old Latin authors, which describe very
analogous cattle diseases, and among them the following :—' Anno 1552 Medicinam faciente in Lucensium
balneis collega meo narrabit *Francisc. de Pergula*, ejus
loci Lucensium nomine Vicarius, ibi circa pagum Mena-
biam supra balnea in fine Maij morbum quendam in-
vasisse pecora tam pestilentem, ut statim corrupta
tumescentia conciderent mortua. Rusticos verò cum id
animadvertissent, quædam, subito affecta, è vestigio
mactasse, in quibus ita erat observatum ut si horum in-
fectorum sanguis nudum contingeret hominis corpus, An-
thraces procrearet, qui (quod mirum erat), non patefacti
erant innoxii : aperti autem et confestim cauterio non
notati latissime serpebant, et aliquibus mortis erant causa.
Caro pecorum recens læsorum et mactatorum cocta co-
mestaque nihil inferebat incommodi : at jus carnis lethale
potanti deprehensum est. Comprimis autem a sanguine
et visceribus talium brutorum cavendum, cum hæc veneni
sint delubra.'

L. C. F. Garmanni, de Miraculis Mortuorum Libri
Tres. Opus Physico Medicum editum a L. J. H. Gar-
manico : Dresdæ et Lipsiæ, M.DCC.IX. 4to. p. 373.

Hezekiah's Disease.—Dr. Green informs me that the
word translated 'lump' (R. V. *cake*) of 'figs' is *d'bhêlah*,
and is generally used without the name of the fruit, this
being implied. The dried figs were pressed together in
the form of a cake, as now, for better keeping. In the
passages relating to Hezekiah, and in these only the
word for figs is added. The meaning cannot possibly
be anything else than a 'cake of figs' (used as a plaster).
There can be no doubt that in this form figs were used
as a remedy, both in ancient and modern times, and that
in certain cases they are both convenient and efficient
forms of poultice. It may be a question what was the
precise nature of the 'burning tumor' of Hezekiah, though

we think the view we have taken that it was a carbuncle is by far the most probable. My friend, Dr. Lauder Brunton, tells me that he has been led to view the disease as 'tonsillitis' from the similarity of the symptoms described by Isaiah with those of some cases of quinsy (tonsillitis). 'In many cases,' says Dr. Brunton, 'that I have seen, the pains in the bones have been so severe as to attract the attention of the patient, to the exclusion of all mention of sore throat.' 'If Hezekiah suffered from tonsillitis his comparison of a lion breaking his bones is a very apt one, and the swelling of the tonsils would also explain the alteration in his speech, which made him " chatter like a crane or a swallow." The dried figs would be almost the only poultice that could be applied to the boil in his fauces, and the rapid maturation of the inflamed boil in the throat affected by the poultice would explain the rapid recovery.'

The Rev. Dr. Adler, the venerable and learned chief Rabbi of the London Synagogue, has kindly favoured me with the following criticisms which will be read with the interest and appreciation which such an authority justly deserves :—

P. 31, concerning *nétheq*. The Mishna in the Treatise on Plagues regards *nétheq*, in accordance with Dr. Green's view, as a scurf on the head, the hairs of which are to be torn. The words, v. 33, 'it shall be shaven' are explained by the Aramaic Targum to mean 'round the spot,' not very near to the spot.

Tradition does not regard *bohaq* as a white eruption, but as a brilliantly shining spot through a mixture of white and red colour. In the Aramaic language we find frequently the verb *bohaq* used so.

P. 36. It is not proved that no cleansing took place with regard to Miriam. The words, Num. xii. 15, 'the people journeyed not till Miriam was brought in again,' may mean that she was cleansed between the time of her shutting in and coming out of the camp.

P. 37. It seems that the leprosy was contagious, because the patient had to cry: ' Unclean, unclean!' when he was brought out of the camp; cf. Deut. xxiv. 8–9. To prevent infection, he had to sit alone, and when his malady was fatal, he was placed in a kind of infirmary, called in Hebrew בֵּית הַחָפְשִׁית (Beth Hachopshith), literally the House of Freedom (free from anxiety to infect others, or because in the same he was taken care for), wherein King Asa dwelt (1 Kings xv. 5 and 2 Chron. xxvi. 21).

P. 41. There is not the least doubt that, when the Temple was standing, the laws of cleanliness were practically carried out. The Mishna in the above-mentioned treatise (14. 13) relates that the Jewish inhabitants of Alexandria asked a question of Rabbi Joshua about two lepers.

P. 42. The question, What was the difference between lepers and non-lepers, since, according to Num. v. 2–4, both are excluded from the camp? is answered in the above-mentioned that the non-lepers were excluded from the portion of the Tabernacle, called the camp of the Levites and Israelites, while the lepers were excluded from the whole camp.

P. 57. Omitted the plague called Ketef קֶטֶב, which A. V. renders ' destruction.' Mentioned four times in the Old Testament—Deut. xxxii. 24, Isa. xxviii. 2, Ps. xci. 6, Hos. xiii. 14.

P. 68. Omitted the pestilence, when the Israelites joined unto Baal-peor (Num. xxv. 9–15).

P. 116. Concerning the passage Eccl. xii. 5. Our commentaries explain it in connection with the former part of the verse about the difficulty the aged experience in walking: ' The almond-tree refuses.' The former celerity which is symbolised by the almond-tree that advances its blossoms before other trees, and is called in Hebrew שָׁקֵד from the same verb *shakod*=hasten: refuses or contradicts from the verb נָאַץ *noaz*; also the following part—' The jumping grasshopper shall become a burden:' the old man is unable to skip or jump.

K

INDEX.

INDEX OF SCRIPTURE REFERENCES.

BY-PATHS OF BIBLE KNOWLEDGE.

"The volumes which the Committee of the Religious Tract Society is issuing under the above title fully deserve success. Most of them have been entrusted to scholars who have a special acquaintance with the subjects about which they severally treat."

The Athenæum.

---

1. **Cleopatra's Needle.** A History of the London Obelisk, with an Exposition of the Hieroglyphics. By the Rev. J. KING, Lecturer for the Palestine Exploration Fund. With Illustrations. Crown 8vo., 2s. 6d. cloth boards.

> "Mr. King's account of the monument seems fairly full and satisfactory."
> *Saturday Review.*
>
> "In every way interestingly written."—*Literary Churchman.*

2. **Fresh Light from the Ancient Monuments.** By A. H. SAYCE, M.A., Deputy Professor of Comparative Philology, Oxford, &c. A sketch of the most striking confirmations of the Bible from recent discoveries in Egypt, Assyria, Babylonia, Palestine, and Asia Minor. With Facsimiles from Photographs. 3s. cloth boards.

> "All who wish to understand the Bible, and all who take an interest in ancient history, ought to procure it."—*Leeds Mercury.*

3. **Recent Discoveries on the Temple Hill at Jerusalem.** By the Rev. J. KING, M.A., Authorised Lecturer for the Palestine Exploration Fund. With Maps, Plans, and Illustrations. 8vo., 2s. 6d. cloth boards.

> "An interesting little book, well deserving of perusal."—*Literary Churchman.*
>
> "An excellent and cheap compendium of information on a subject of intense and perpetual interest."—*Watchman.*

4. **Babylonian Life and History.** By E. A. WALLIS BUDGE, B.A., Camb., Assistant in the Department of Oriental Antiquities, British Museum. Illustrated. Crown 8vo., 3s., cloth boards.

> "An admirable addition to this excellent series of 'By-Paths of Bible Knowledge.' Mr. Budge's method is sound, and his book is worthy of his reputation."
> *Saturday Review.*
>
> "A very readable little book, which tells the general reader all he need care to know about the life of the old people of Chaldea."—*Athenæum.*

5. **Galilee in the Time of Christ.** By SELAH MERRILL, D.D., author of "East of the Jordan," etc. With a Map. Crown 8vo., 2s. 6d. cloth boards.

> "Will be of great service to all who desire to realise the actual surroundings amid which our Lord spent His life on earth, and will be specially useful in correcting some false notions which have obtained wide currency, *e.g.*, the common idea that Nazareth was a small, obscure, and immoral place."
> *Congregationalist.*

6. Egypt and Syria. Their Physical Features in Relation to Bible History. By Sir J. W. DAWSON, F.G.S., F.R.S., President of the British Association, 1886. Crown 8vo., 3s. cloth boards.

"This is one of the most interesting of the series to which it belongs. It is the result of personal observation, and the work of a practised geological observer. . . . The questions raised in this little volume are discussed in the light of the most advanced knowledge and of large scientific faculty, and at the same time with great religious reverence."—*British Quarterly Review.*

"We know of nothing at all comparable to it as giving a succinct, clear, and constantly instructive account of the geological features of Egypt and Syria in their relations to the Bible, by the hand of a practised geologist."—*Record.*

7. Assyria : Its Princes, Priests, and People. By A. H. SAYCE, M.A., LL.D., author of " Fresh Light from Ancient Monuments," " Introduction to Ezra, Nehemiah, and Esther," &c. Illustrated. 3s. cloth boards.

"A little masterpiece. it presents with scientific accuracy, and yet in a thoroughly popular form, all that is of most essential significance in the realised information respecting that old-world history and life."—*Christian Leader.*

8. The Dwellers by the Nile. Chapters on the Life, Literature, History, and Customs of Ancient Egypt. By E. A. WALLIS BUDGE, M.A., Assistant in Department of Oriental Antiquities, British Museum. Crown 8vo., cloth boards. With many illustrations. 3s. cloth.

"A little book that contains a vast amount of information respecting that historic land, Egypt. . . . The history and explanation of the hieroglyphics and the discovery of their interpretation is lucidly and ably told."—*Times.*

9. The Diseases of the Bible. By Sir J. RISDON BENNETT, Ex-President of the Royal College of Physicians. 2s. 6d. cloth.

Sir Risdon Bennett has studied all the references in the Bible to diseases of various kinds in the light of the fullest and best knowledge of the present state of medical science. Such subjects as leprosy, demoniacal possession, etc., are carefully considered ; and it cannot but be a great help to intelligent study of the Bible to have the latest scientific view of these and kindred subjects.

"We cannot too thoroughly commend this work, both on account of the subjects of which it treats, and for its intrinsic literary worth."
Provincial Medical Journal.

"An entertaining and instructive volume, written in simple untechnical language for the general reader."—*Christian World.*

10. Trees and Plants of the Bible. By W. H. GROSER, B.Sc. Illustrated. 3s. cloth boards.

"A useful little volume for Bible teachers and readers."—*Saturday Review.*

"Apart from its religious value, this little volume must approve itself to all lovers of botany."—*Times (Weekly Edition.)*

"There is no book on the subject which contains so much of the best information packed into so small a compass."—*Christian Leader.*

(OTHER VOLUMES ARE IN PREPARATION.)